THE CLASSICAL ORDERS OF ARCHITECTURE

Dedicated to the memory of Cecil Burns, Architect, who introduced me to the work of James Gibbs and taught me how to set out the entasis of columns.

THE CLASSICAL ORDERS OF ARCHITECTURE

SECOND EDITION

ROBERT CHITHAM

Incorporating James Gibbs and the American
Classical Tradition, by Calder Loth

ELSEVIER

AMSTERDAM • BOSTON • HEIDELBERG • LONDON • NEW YORK • OXFORD
PARIS • SAN DIEGO • SAN FRANCISCO • SINGAPORE • SYDNEY • TOKYO

Architectural Press is an imprint of Elsevier

Architectural
Press

Architectural Press
An imprint of Elsevier
Linacre House, Jordan Hill, Oxford OX2 8DP
30 Corporate Drive, Burlington, MA 01803

First published 1985
Second edition 2005

Permissions may be sought directly from Elsevier's Science and Technology
Rights Department in Oxford, UK: phone: (+44) (0) 1865 843830; fax: (+44)
(0) 1865 853333; e-mail: permissions@elsevier.co.uk. You may also complete
your request on-line via the Elsevier homepage (http://www.elsevier.com),
by selecting 'Customer Support' and then 'Obtaining Permissions'

British Library Cataloguing in Publication Data
A catalogue record for this book is available from the British Library

ISBN 0 7506 61240

For information about all Architectural Press publications
visit our website at http://books.elsevier.com/architecturalpress

Typeset by Newgen Imaging Systems (P) Ltd., Chennai, India
Printed and bound in Great Britain

CONTENTS

FOREWORD, BY PETER HODSON

PREFACE TO THE SECOND EDITION

INTRODUCTION

HISTORICAL BACKGROUND

Plates 1–3 The Greek Orders: Doric, Ionic and Corinthian   29
Plate 4 Comparative Tuscan Orders   36
Plate 5 Comparative Doric Orders   39
Plate 6 Comparative Ionic Orders   42
Plate 7 Comparative Corinthian Orders   45
Plate 8 Comparative Composite Orders   48

THE ORDERS IN DETAIL

Plate 9 The Five Orders   53
Plate 10 The Tuscan Order   56
Plate 11 The Tuscan Capital and Entablature   58
Plate 12 The Tuscan Base and Pedestal   60
Plate 13 The Doric Order   62
Plate 14 The Doric Capital and Entablature I   64
Plate 15 The Doric Capital and Entablature II   67
Plate 16 The Doric Base and Pedestal   68
Plate 17 The Ionic Order   70
Plate 18 The Ionic Volute   72
Plate 19 The Ionic Capital and Entablature   74
Plate 20 The Ionic Capital I   76

Plate 21 The Ionic Capital II   79
Plate 22 The Ionic Base and Pedestal   80
Plate 23 The Corinthian Order   82
Plate 24 The Corinthian Capital and Entablature   84
Plate 25 The Corinthian Entablature   86
Plate 26 The Corinthian Capital   88
Plate 27 The Corinthian Base and Pedestal   90
Plate 28 The Composite Order   92
Plate 29 The Composite Capital and Entablature   94
Plate 30 The Composite Entablature   96
Plate 31 The Composite Capital   98
Plate 32 The Composite Base and Pedestal   100
Plate 33 Comparison of Mouldings   102

JAMES GIBBS AND THE
AMERICAN CLASSICAL TRADITION

Plate 34   James Gibbs, design for a round window, plate 110, *A Book of Architecture*
            (RIBA Library Photographs Collection)   105
Plate 35a   James Gibbs, design for the west front of St Martin's in the Fields,
            plate 3, *A Book of Architecture* (RIBA Library Photographs Collection)   109
Plate 35b   James Gibbs, design for a garden seat, Plate 82, *A Book of Architecture*
            (RIBA Library Photographs Collection)   111
Plate 35c   Christ Church, Philadelphia (Historic American Buildings Survey)   111
Plate 35d   St. Paul's Chapel, New York City (Historic American Buildings Survey)   111
Plate 36a   First Congregational Church, Litchfield, Connecticut
            (Historic American Buildings Survey)   113
Plate 36b   First Congregational Church, New Haven, Connecticut
            (Historic American Buildings Survey)   114
Plate 37a   James Gibbs, design for a gentleman in Dorsetshire, plate 58, *A Book of
            Architecture* (RIBA Library Photographs Collection)   115
Plate 37b   Mount Airy, Richmond County, Virginia
            (Historic American Buildings Survey)   115
Plate 38a   Hammond-Harwood House, Annapolis, Maryland
            (Historic American Buildings Survey)   117
Plate 38b   James Gibbs, designs for niches, plate 109, *A Book of Architecture*
            (RIBA Library Photographs Collection)   117
Plate 38c   James Gibbs, design for a gentleman in Yorkshire, plate 63, *A Book of
            Architecture* (RIBA Library Photographs Collection)   118
Plate 38d   John Hawks, design for Tryon Palace, New Bern, North Carolina
            (Courtesy of Tryon Palace Historic Sites and Gardens, North Carolina
            Department of Cultural Resources)   118

Plate 39a Elisha Sheldon House, Litchfield, Connecticut
(Historic American Buildings Survey) 120
Plate 39b James Gibbs, draught made for a house for a Gentleman in 1720,
plate 43, *A Book of Architecture* (RIBA Library Photographs Collection) 120
Plate 40a John Edwards House, Charleston, South Carolina
(Historic American Buildings Survey) 122
Plate 40b James Gibbs, 'The Ionick Capital,' plate XIV, *Rules for Drawing*
(RIBA Library Photographs Collection) 122
Plate 41a James Gibbs, design for a temple in the Doric order, plate 67,
A Book of Architecture (RIBA Library Photographs Collection) 124
Plate 41b Monticello, Albemarle County, Virginia (Robert C. Lautman,
Courtesy of The Thomas Jefferson Foundation) 124
Plate 42a James Gibbs, design for a house at Seacomb Park, plate 53, *A Book of
Architecture* (RIBA Library Photographs Collection) 126
Plate 42b James Hoban, N. elevation, The White House, Washington, D.C.
(Maryland Historical Society) 126
Plate 43a James Gibbs, design for a house to be built in Greenwich, plate 47,
A Book of Architecture (RIBA Library Photographs Collection) 129
Plate 43b Whitemarsh Hall (destroyed), Wyndmoor, Pennsylvania
(Pennsylvania State Archives) 129
Plate 44 Milburne, Richmond, Virginia (Calder Loth) 131

THE 96-PART ORDERS

Plate 45 The Five Orders, After James Gibbs 137
Plate 46 The Tuscan Order 140
Plate 47 The Tuscan Capital and Entablature 142
Plate 48 The Tuscan Base and Pedestal 143
Plate 49 The Doric Order 144
Plate 50 The Doric Capital and Entablature 146
Plate 51 The Doric Base and pedestal 147
Plate 52 The Ionic Order 148
Plate 53 The Ionic Capital and Entablature 150
Plate 54 The Ionic Base and Pedestal 151
Plate 55 The Corinthian Order 152
Plate 56 The Corinthian Capital and Entablature 154
Plate 57 The Corinthian Base and Pedestal 155
Plate 58 The Composite Order 156
Plate 59 The Composite Capital and Entablature 158
Plate 60 The Composite Base and Pedestal 159

USE OF THE ORDERS

Plate 61	The Column: Diminution and Fluting	163
Plate 62	Intercolumniation I: Tuscan and Ionic	166
Plate 63	Intercolumniation II: Doric, Corinthian and Composite	168
Plate 64	Arches I: Without Pedestals	171
Plate 65	Arches II: With Pedestals	174
Plate 66	Arches III: Details	176
Plate 67	Balustrades	179
Plate 68	Superimposed Orders I and II	182
Plate 69	Superimposed Orders I and II	185
Plate 70	Attics and Basements I and II	186
Plate 71	Attics and Basements I and II	189
Plate 72	Rustication	190
Plate 73	Pediments	193
Plate 74	Doors and Windows I	196
Plate 75	Doors and Windows II	198
Plate 76	Mouldings and Their Enrichment	200
Plate 77	Characteristics of Classicism	203

ILLUSTRATED GLOSSARY

BIBLIOGRAPHY

FOREWORD

When Robert Chitham first published his *The Classical Orders of Architecture* in 1985, the timing could hardly have been better for a new drawing-board manual for delineating the orders and mastering the essentials of the Classical language, designed for practical, day-to-day use by modern practitioners. In the previous year, the Prince of Wales had thrown down the gauntlet to the hitherto virtually unchallenged Modernist architectural establishment, in his celebrated Hampton Court speech to the 100th anniversary dinner of the Royal Institute of British Architects. The frequent acrimony of the ensuing 'style wars' of the 1980s and 1990s resolved little, but HRH's interventions unquestionably raised the work of Classical architects from obscurity and wilful neglect into a subject for serious public interest and debate. Those already engaged in designing or teaching in the Classical language, and others who now felt free to do so, welcomed Chitham's work.

Soon after its publication, I began to use Chitham as the teaching textbook for my 'Introduction To The Classical Language of Architecture' course at the Portsmouth School of Architecture, which focused, as traditionally, on the necessity of actually drawing the orders as the beginning of wisdom. Since 1977, when it was initiated, I had used Palladio in the Placzec facsimile edition of the Ware translation. Palladio's orders are perhaps unequalled in their beauty, subtlety and influence, but the antiquated text and confusing plates, set about with tiny numbers bristling with fractions which never-quite-clearly refer to the dimensions of particular parts, was not the ideal vehicle for introducing second-year architectural students, innocent of any previous experience of it, to 'basic literacy' in the Classical orders.

Not only did Chitham's primary innovation of dividing the module – the lower diameter of the column shaft of an order, of which the dimensions of all other parts of the order are multiples or fractions – into 100 parts, instead of the traditional 30 or 60, make calculation and dimensioning in metric measurements simple, but also his sequential method of building up the order as you draw it meant that students virtually taught themselves, much the best way. Equally invaluable were the clear expositions of the vocabulary, grammar and syntax of all the essential elements of the Classical language, the unique comparison plates of ideal orders from the Masters, and, not least, the fine metric orders of Chitham's own invention themselves, which now take their rightful place in the canon after Gibbs and Chambers.

Meanwhile, the Prince of Wales had established his Institute of Architecture in 1992 to promote his traditional, classical and counter-Modernist architectural views; centring on a

Foundation Course providing an introduction to these aspects, largely untaught elsewhere, to would-be architects and others. Hugh Petter, a former Portsmouth student who had become the POWIA's Foundation Course Senior Tutor, invited me to do my 'Introduction To The Classical Language' course there in 1994, and it remained a staple, with Robert Chitham as both text and, personally, as a tutor until the demise of the Institute in 2001. Also in 1994, I was asked to provide my course in another venue, where the Chitham book as it stood was not able to provide me with the same all-encompassing teaching text.

This new venue was in the United States; more specifically the School of the Arts of Virginia Commonwealth University in Richmond, which invited me to set up and teach a summer course, 'Introduction To The Classical Language', aimed at students and practitioners in architecture and architectural history, interior design, historic preservation and at interested laymen. This course would have to address the needs of students with little or no experience of the Classical of drawing. The Chitham method proved ideal for this purpose too, but one completely essential thing his orders were not, and that was in feet and inches, America remaining stubbornly (and rightly) duodecimal.

In addition to converting his method for drawing the orders to a base-twelve division of the module, my challenge to Robert Chitham was to apply both method and new module to the orders of James Gibbs, these being far and away the orders most used in Virginia, particularly in its colonial past, and the ones whose general form and appearance were most familiar to its inhabitants. Chitham's response was to devise a new modular division of 96 parts – again, instead of the traditional 30 or 60 – and, with the assistance of Christopher Cotton, another former Portsmouth student, he set about converting the dimensions of Gibbs's orders from the original proportional notations to numerical, rendered in dimensions of multiples or parts of the 96-part module. This proved wonderfully effective, and as successful in minimising the appearance in the dimensions of the dreaded fractions as Gibbs had boasted his proportional method to be.

There has been some historical debate, particularly in America, over the relative merits of proportional or numerical, modular methods of proportioning the orders, and some have asked, why not just use Gibbs's orders in their original format? My belief was that for non-professionals, or even professionals to whom the Classical was largely terra incognita, numbers, rather than proportional relationships, would be more quickly accessible, and so it has proven. In a culture with a duodecimal measuring system, familiar to all from earliest childhood schooling, along with the concomitant concepts of halves, thirds, quarters, sixths and twelfths, the proportional relationships of the parts of a 96-part module order (virtually all cleanly multipliable or divisible by 2, 3, 4, 6 and 12) would be readily apparent.

To our great satisfaction, the first VCU students in the hot June of 1994, some of whom had never so much as drawn a line using drawing board and parallel, took to the new system at once. In this and subsequent years, computer-generation students devised useful calculator methods, which made short work of the numbers, but many found that they needed no more than a simple ruler and the ability to count. Architects, to whom I was later to offer the course for professional continuing education purposes, proved, for the most part, even quicker students; once the 'Helen Keller moment' had occurred – the realisation that the key to the Classical was a modular dimension of which all parts of an order, and the building to which the order is applied, are either multiples or fractions – they were away.

Now, nearly two decades on from its original publication, the need for a new edition of Robert Chitham's *The Classical Orders of Architecture* is perhaps even more compelling than it was in 1985. True, in Britain, an uneasy truce obtains between the Modernist and Classical camps, and Classical architects, such as Robert Adam, Quinlan Terry, John Simpson, Julien Bicknell and Demitri Porphyrios, have successful practices, and, despite sporadic sniper fire from the usual ideological redoubts, their work is seriously reviewed. The indefatigable Robert Adam has brought about the formation of a Traditional Architecture Group within the RIBA membership; its first meeting attracted an astonishing turnout of over 200, and, under Adam's leadership, it is rapidly establishing itself as a forceful advocacy forum for non-modernist architecture, in both practice and education, from within the very bastion of the British architectural establishment itself. Its name does not, however, include the contentious word 'Classical', which, in the highly-charged atmosphere of New Labour Britain, is perhaps only prudent.

No such inhibitions constrain America, it seems, where the dynamic Institute of Classical Architecture of New York has celebrated its tenth anniversary with a sumptuous volume of new American classical architecture. Its journal, *The Classicist* annually features ever-increasing contributions to its 'From The Practices' and 'From The Academies' sections, showing a thriving, nationwide Classical design culture in practice and in education. This has been fed in the former by the Institute's own courses for practitioners out of New York (now to be franchised on a regional basis) and in the latter by University schools of architecture like Notre Dame (so far the only exclusively classical and traditional school) and a growing number of others offering Classical programmes, such as Miami, under Richard John.

On the education front in Britain, Portsmouth (whilst by no means a traditionalist school by ethos) remains, so far as I am aware, the only architecture school in which 'basic literacy' in the Classical is a course requirement. This situation is being addressed as we write, however, by Robert Adam and Hugh Petter, who have begun to take the Classical 'on the road' to other schools where the light shineth not yet. It must also be mentioned that, in the age of the Internet, Classical and Traditional architecture enthusiasts, like all other devotees of minority interests, may now converse and organise via the Tradarch site in America (now under the aegis of the Institute of Classical Architecture) and INTBAU out of the new Prince's Foundation in London.

All of this is highly gratifying to the community of Classicists, but a major lacuna still exists in the contemporary teaching and practice of Classical architecture, and that is the problem of literacy. Andres Duany has said that the great enemy of traditional architecture today is not bad modern and modernists but bad classical and classicists. Calder Loth, in these pages, and in his highly successful courses in architectural literacy in Richmond, Virginia, has forcefully pointed out that not only is much new classical design illiterate, but that the very concept that there is such a thing as literacy in Classical design (and that it matters) is conspicuously absent; occasionally even from the work of traditionalist architects of repute who apparently believe the Classical can be got right merely by judicious eye-balling. Loth says: 'No architect would allow a sloppy, mis-spelt or ungrammatical letter to go out to clients from his office; why then an illiterate Classical design?' It is not only the architecture and design professions, however, which must be apprised of the necessity of Classical literacy, but also – as was James Gibbs's own ambition in the early 18th century – the non-architect developers and builders of speculative housing, and the individual and institutional commissioners of classical buildings who are their clients.

With the publication of this new, revised and expanded edition of Robert Chitham's *The Classical Orders of Architecture*, including the 96-part-module Gibbs orders, there can be no excuse for any architectural practitioner, school or client to be lacking the necessary literacy to design, teach or commission good Classical architecture. And there is but one, time-tested, way to achieve 'basic literacy' in the Classical language of architecture; all that is needed to do it is to be found in this book:

NOW GO AND DRAW THE ORDERS.

Peter Hodson
Senior Lecturer, University of Portsmouth School of Architecture

'Metiendo Vivendum'
('By Measure We Live' – Motto of Sir Edwin Lutyens, greatest of modern Classicists)

PREFACE TO THE SECOND EDITION

The first edition of *The Classical Orders of Architecture*, published in 1985, set out to simplify the traditional method of proportioning the orders. By studying a number of historical treatises, a set of 'ideal' orders was developed. These were then proportioned, using the diameter of the column above its base as a module. Unlike previous examples, which commonly divided the module into 30 or 60 parts, proportions of the elements of the orders were then defined as decimal fractions of the module. The purpose of this method of proportioning was to avoid the use of unmanageable fractions, and at the same time to make it easy to use a calculator to determine dimensions.

This proved a popular system, particularly for those teaching the orders to students. Those hitherto baffled by the arithmetic of the orders could draw them with sufficient ease to be able to concentrate on the broader problems of the use of classical architectural grammar. The book in translation found a market in Germany, and – to my great joy – in Italy.

In his foreword Peter Hodson explains the genesis of this second edition, with its parallel 96-part orders added to the metric orders of the original. When he mooted the idea of a non-metric canon, the image I had was of the traditional school ruler, with 12 inches divided into eighths. I thought that perhaps the orders could be proportioned by means of major parts of the module (twelfths), divided into minor parts (eighths of twelfths, or ninety-sixths of the module). Chris Cotton undertook the initial task of converting all the proportions in the original plates into 96-part notation.

In fact these proportions did not prove amenable to subdivision into major and minor parts, and the second set of orders now published discards the method as cumbersome and irrelevant. Not surprisingly, the orders published in James Gibbs's *Rules for Drawing the Several Parts of Architecture* proved more amenable to 96-part notation than my decimal orders, presumably because of their fractional arrangement as well as the essentially feet-and-inches perspective of their author.

I set out with the intention of reproducing the original set of plates, amended to show the 96-part notation developed by Chris Cotton. However, because of the great influence of James Gibbs on American architecture of the 18th century, an emphasis on Gibbs seemed appropriate. Calder Loth, of the Virginia Department of Historic Resources, was persuaded to write for the book the essay on Gibbs, and at the same time I agreed that my second parallel should be based not on the 'ideal' order developed for the first edition but on the orders set out in Gibbs's *Rules*.

In converting Gibbs's fractions (and fractions of fractions), I used computer-aided drafting for the initial setting-out of the orders, though the actual plates in the book were drawn by hand. (The first edition was of course completed before the use of CAD became universal.) In constructing the orders this way, I became aware of course that what had been found in 1985 to be appropriate for the pocket calculator is equally appropriate for the computer. Indeed, the computer is so good at dividing lengths into fractions that it is perfectly easy to draw the orders direct from Gibbs's *Rules*. To that extent, my reworking of Gibbs may seem superfluous, but it does have the advantage that it presents all the proportions of the orders according to a single comprehensible scale, as well as picking up one or two minor anomalies in Gibbs's original work. Moreover, its use makes it easy to avoid unduly complicated fractional dimensions.

Moreover, the use of CAD proved a powerful asset both in checking the arithmetic of the new proportions, and in solving two hitherto somewhat intractable problems, the setting-out of the volute and the scotia. The volute is a stern test of draftsmanship because of its dependence on a high level of accuracy in striking the centres of its component quadrants. Finding the centre of the lower arc of the scotia is a trigonometrical puzzle that Cotton has solved but that I in the end preferred to circumvent.

The book therefore offers readers (on both sides of the Atlantic) a choice of two sets of orders. The variations between them are not for the most part great. But in one significant respect Gibbs (and Palladio) depart from the models I chose for proportioning my orders. This is in the proportion of entablature to column in the 'major' orders – Ionic, Corinthian and Composite. Gibbs's deliberate reduction of the scale of the entablature in these orders produces a lighter balance, which is more apparent in a building as a whole than in its constituent orders. Some may find this preferable to the emphasis on the entablature prescribed by Chambers and others, which I adopted for my original 'ideal'.

In all respects the 96-part orders are shown in the same way as those with 100 parts.

In presenting this book I acknowledge gratefully the advocacy of Peter Hodson, the painstaking re-calculation of the proportions by Chris Cotton, and the elegant contribution of Calder Loth, as well as the efforts of my colleagues Julia Nicholson and John Bridges, for transcribing my manuscript scribbling and converting my manual efforts into material suitable for the age of the computer.

INTRODUCTION

THE TEACHING OF THE ORDERS

The first half of the twentieth century saw a gradual decline in the knowledge and use of the classical orders in architectural practice. Up to the early 1900s nearly all architects possessed a practical familiarity with classical architecture, that is to say architecture derived from ancient Greece and Rome, but this familiarity diminished as the Modern Movement became established.

The origins and causes of the Modern Movement lie far beyond the scope of this book, but it is relevant to observe an apparent paradox in its philosophy. It is a characteristic of modern design that it deliberately eschews overtly historical form on the grounds that the historical seams have been fully worked out, have become sterile and are incapable of further inventive development. At the same time, modern architecture is held to be inspired in an abstract sense by its classical forebears. The writings of Modern Movement architects repeatedly attest to classical architecture as the intellectual basis of their work.

During the slow ascendancy of the Modern Movement before and just after the Second World War, the formal teaching of the orders persisted, partly because of the classical training of many of the teachers themselves and partly on account of this identification of classicism as the background of modern work. The grip of neo-classicism, although faltering, was thus not immediately broken, surviving far longer in the field of architecture than in the companion arts less beholden to the public taste. While the schools continued to teach the minutiae of the orders, architectural competitions continued to attract entries in classical styles and major classical buildings continued to be built. There was no lack of fluency in the orders; expertise in their manipulation was not only formally absorbed by students in the schools, but handed on by the system of individual pupilage. This knowledge was supplemented by a continuous flow of information from books and periodicals including both projects and measured drawings.

It must be said that a large proportion of the classical work of the time is weary and repetitious, having all the hallmarks of a style in decay. The growing confidence of the Modern Movement must have made it difficult for the architect of average competence to pursue classical solutions with anything of the certainty of his Edwardian predecessors. But in the midst of this retreat the designs of a few architects, in particular of Lutyens, stand out to deny the charge that classicism could no longer be seriously explored.

It was not until the 1950s that, in the United Kingdom at least, classicism suffered virtually total eclipse. While in a number of schools the teaching of the orders as an academic exercise continued, the submission of classical solutions to competitions came to be regarded with derision. Side by side with this lapse of interest the previous wealth of printed material disappeared from view. The parallels of the orders went out of print, and the information made available by the technical press languished on the reference library shelves.

Modern educationalists relegated books on classical architecture to a place in the history syllabus, quite divorced from the practical everyday business of design. Post-war architecture having set its face bravely against derivation from historical sources, there seemed no purpose in keeping up the old, detailed knowledge. With the exception of one or two individuals and practices, working either in the restoration of historic buildings or the design of buildings for occasional clients of antiquarian tastes, few architects in practice would claim to have an intimate working knowledge of the five orders.

At the same time, the 1950s and 1960s saw, in Europe as elsewhere, the greatest volume of new building construction ever undertaken. The reconstruction of towns and cities devastated by war combined with an unprecedented increase in prosperity to produce a massive boom in building. The Modern Movement, springing from a context of industrial expansion and the decay of craft work, might have been assumed to be made for this moment. But in a curious way it proved inappropriate to meet the challenge. The great architects of the thirties, searching for a kind of purity of expression, stripped their work of extraneous decoration and even surface texture, employing a refinement of form which appealed almost exclusively to the intellect.

But whereas the wealth and diversity of historical styles had previously equipped the architectural profession at large with sufficient means to produce designs of a generally acceptable level of competence, the deliberately restricted vocabulary of the Modern Movement was too sophisticated in essence for any but the most gifted to exploit with assurance. Comparatively few architects were capable of such intellectual rigour, so whilst many fine buildings were produced, the demand for greatly increased quantity of new building led inevitably to a loss of quality.

Moreover, while a scatter of modern buildings on specific sites of dramatic aspect or amongst a multitude of more traditional architecture produced considerable visual excitement, once such buildings came to be concentrated, in the centre of re-constructed cities or in the vast housing developments necessitated by slum clearance, the lack of contrast and incident became apparent. It became clear, in fact, that the Modern Movement was to a great extent architects' architecture. If so many practising architects could make so little of the sophistication of the Modern Movement, the general public could make even less. But architecture is a wholly public art, and the architect has a responsibility not shared by other artists to the public at large. It may be the function of the artist to lead fashion and to mould taste. But the architect must beware of leading fashion by so great a distance that he and the rest of society part company. Whatever their intellectual pretensions, people attach more importance to buildings than perhaps to other art forms, and because they regard buildings as long-lived, and thus as symbols of stability, they tend to be conservative in their architectural taste. The effect of rapid and wholesale redevelopment in the immediate post-war period was to demonstrate, first, that on the whole people reacted against too great a rate of change in the built environment, and, second, that they were not uniformly enthusiastic about the physical appearance of the results of all this activity, however much their actual working or living environment might be improved. It was primarily outrage at the scale of destruction of the old and disappointment with the quality of the new that prompted the enormous surge of popular interest in conservation towards the end of the 1960s, rather than any objective interest in historical style. The result of the outcry, however, was the retention of a far greater proportion of old buildings than had seemed probable in the recent past. But if old buildings had to be preserved and retained in use, they had to be repaired, restored and modernised, so there followed a shift of emphasis in the building industry from new construction to rehabilitation. If this expanding programme of rehabilitation were to be carried on with sensitivity, some knowledge of the original design and construction of the buildings concerned was clearly desirable.

In the centres of cities, where great concentrations of buildings of historic interest are to be found, an overwhelming proportion is of classical design. A single example will serve to illustrate this. Every weekday I walk to my office from Charing Cross Station, a walk of some fifteen minutes. I have counted the buildings I pass, and find that there are one hundred and sixteen identifiably separate façades lining my route – some are single houses whilst others occupy anything up to a complete street block. Of these hundred and sixteen, no fewer than ninety-four can be unequivocally classified as overtly classical or derived from classical sources. Discounting ground storey features such as doorcases and shopfronts, some fourteen or fifteen have expressed classical orders, while the remainder exhibit a profusion of cornices, pediments, strip pilasters, aedicular orders around windows and other essentially classical features.

While such a striking concentration is not to be taken as the norm for urban landscape as a whole, it is by no means unusual. Many parts of Central London and the centres of other cities and towns would if similarly analysed yield results showing similar characteristics. The fact is, our predecessors have left us a huge legacy of classical architecture which, despite the massive redevelopment programmes of recent decades, still shapes the character of our towns and cities to a significant extent. Therefore, such is now the importance of rehabilitation and refurbishment work that even if no more new classical buildings were ever to be attempted, the maintenance, repair, restoration and extension of the existing building stock demands of architects some knowledge of the vocabulary of classicism if such work is to be carried out in a literate manner.

That is not all, though. For on the heels of the conservation movement, and the resultant requirement for expertise in the refurbishment of existing buildings, has appeared an even more unexpected phenomenon. Gradually, interest is reviving in the design of new buildings in historically derived styles. Techniques preserved with dogged perseverance by a handful are beginning to be required of a widening circle of architects. Architectural design today appears to be moving in a number of different directions at the same time, and side by side with the latest expositions of contemporary forms are appearing buildings of recognisable stylistic ancestry. No one can say where this re-examination of stylistic architecture will lead, but it seems clear that some architects, some of the time, once again need some kind of guidance in the language of the classical orders.

Those few who have never forsaken classical design need no such help, and this book is not directed at them. But it does seem that there is now a place for a new, straightforward handbook of the orders to refresh older memories as well as to assist those to whom the subject is new.

Why is such guidance needed? We may flatter ourselves that we have a broad general knowledge of historical styles, and of the way the orders are fitted together, sufficient to produce a passable solution to a given problem. If the worst comes to the worst, we can blow the dust off Banister Fletcher – surely all the orders are in there somewhere.

The truth is that the classical orders are not susceptible to so casual an imitation. Individually, each order is constructed of a series of components standing in a clear, though not immutable, proportional relationship with one another, and peculiar to that order. At the same time the orders are closely related to one another by a further series of mathematical progressions and by the manner in which their component mouldings are developed from the simplest order to the most complex. Thus, the orders as a whole form a complete system analogous to a language, abiding by rules of grammar and syntax, capable of being used in a literate manner, but vulnerable to illiterate abuse. The grammatical rules of the orders can be emphasised, elided or distorted for a particular purpose, but the dramatic or poetic effect of such manipulation cannot be more than superficial unless the grammatical rules have first been mastered. Like a language, the orders are capable of development in the long term, but they remain recognisably the same throughout the centuries of their development. The origin, purpose and history of the orders is so comprehensively traced by Sir John Summerson in *The Classical Language of Architecture* that nothing that could be encompassed by this book could be more than the merest imitation. Nor is its scope broad enough to include the vast subject of the application of the orders to classical design, although the final plate, which may be seen as a kind of coda, is a tentative statement of what I believe to be the ruling characteristics of classicism. This book is consciously more limited in scope, a primer rather than a commentary.

Summerson says, 'It is a mistake ever to think of the five orders of architecture as a sort of child's box of bricks which architects have used to save themselves the trouble of inventing. It is much better to think of them as grammatical expressions imposing a formidable discipline within which personal sensibility always has certain play – a discipline moreover which can sometimes be burst asunder by a flight of poetic genius.'[1] This book is concerned with delineating the framework of discipline which Summerson describes. It makes no claim to break new ground, beyond the rationalisation of the system of measurement. Its purpose is to restate the grammar of the orders in a manner which makes them immediately available to the designer.

ROMAN AND RENAISSANCE THEORISTS

In compiling a new book of the orders, the fundamental question to be decided is whether the orders given should be taken from built examples, from the 'ideal' orders of individual authorities, or from the evaluation of a cross-section of earlier work.

Parallels of the orders – the best recent one is Professor Cordingley's edition of *Normand* published by Tiranti – generally consist of a combination of plates, including idealised

---

1. Sir John Summerson, *The Classical Language of Architecture*, p. 13.

orders prepared by Renaissance authorities, and actual measured examples. Individual authorities often restrict their plates to their own ideal versions of the orders, and these are generally derived either from an earlier authority, or direct from a specific example of Roman origin. For this book, I decided against the inclusion of specific Roman examples. For one thing, the measurement of ancient buildings is open to wide variations in interpretation, not least because the draftsman is trapped within the drawing conventions of his own age, as the study of different attempts to record the same building shows clearly.[2] Besides, many of these examples are relatively accessible, and I felt in no way qualified to improve on the measured examples set out in, say, *Normand*.

I decided, therefore, to confine the book to what is in effect my own series of 'ideal' orders – these, clearly, had to be distilled from idealised orders of the past. The whole progress of the Renaissance from its inception was punctuated by treatises on the orders, and I thought it would be most instructive, as a basis for determining a system of proportion of my own, to redraw the orders as set out by a number of these authorities. I had not seen this done before, and was not aware before I began of the extent to which they would vary. The first thing was to choose which of the many authorities to study in this way. In practice this was not difficult, as there is a recognisable stream of thought running through the Renaissance, the Italian authorities who most influenced English Renaissance architecture being readily identified. Any analysis of this kind must in my view begin with Vitruvius. Marcus Vitruvius Pollio was a Roman architect working in the reign of the Emperor Augustus who dedicated to the Emperor his comprehensive book on architecture and building, *De Architectura*. We know nothing of his career or of the buildings he designed, but his book is remarkable for its scope, dealing with all sorts of aspects of town planning, public health, building materials, construction, astronomy and astrology and the design of engines of war. The core of the book is a dissertation on the orders of architecture. Vitruvius deals at length with their proportions and the design of their components, and with the manner in which they are to be used in different kinds of buildings. He groups together the Doric, Ionic and Corinthian as the three major orders, and treats the Tuscan separately, as a kind of rustic curiosity. Throughout his description of the orders, Vitruvius constantly refers to their Greek ancestry. Whether or not he or his contemporaries visited Greece itself, they had sufficient evidence of Greek classical architecture in Southern Italy and Sicily, and they were in no doubt as to the significance of the Greek contribution to the development of classical architecture. Vitruvius is the only Roman architectural text to have been preserved, and though scholars have subsequently scoffed at his pedestrian style or pompous turn of phrase, we are extraordinarily fortunate that the only survivor should be such a comprehensive and cogent treatise.

Indeed, so comprehensive was Vitruvius that he became a kind of yardstick for the early Renaissance writers. There is no doubt that the first great Renaissance treatise, *De Re Aedificatoria*, written by Leone Battista Alberti (1404–72), is very much modelled on the style and content of the Roman work. *De Re Aedificatoria* again consists of ten books, and displays the same breadth of treatment as its Roman progenitor. The orders are described in meticulous detail, and it contains the earliest identification of the Composite as a separate order.

2. Robert Chitham, *Measured Drawing for Architects*, p. 7.

19

The first comprehensive, illustrated handbook of the orders, however, is that of Sebastiano Serlio (1475–1552), and I have chosen Serlio as the first of my Renaissance authorities. His five part *Book of Architecture*, published from 1537 onwards, includes the first plate ever to show the orders together for comparison; he uses this plate as an introduction to his fourth book, in which the five orders are described in great detail, and illustrated by a lively anthology of examples drawn from the antique as well as from his own imagination. Serlio is the first great codifier of the orders, and it is perhaps curious that his comparative frontispiece goes only half way towards identifying the nature of their progression, the five orders being represented somewhat at random, with neither the overall height nor the column diameter being constant.

Serlio, torn between loyalty to the precepts of Vitruvius and a desire for a steady progression in the proportions of the orders, produces a series which as the plates show appear squat to our eyes. In the work of my next Italian authorities the 'ideal' orders, so to speak, reach their full maturity. Giacomo da Vignola (1507–73) published his *Regole delle Cinque Ordini d'Architettura* in 1562, and Andrea Palladio (1508–80) his *I Quattro Libri dell'Architettura* some eight years later. Vignola's work, with its copper engravings of fine quality, insists on a carefully worked out relationship of all the parts in each order. Palladio, with equal brevity of text, lumps together in his first book descriptions of the orders and various notes on construction and building materials. He seems in a hurry to get on to what he regards as the much more interesting matter of the application of the orders, examples of which both from antiquity and from his own *oeuvre* occupy the bulk of the book. Palladio is of particular significance for the English Renaissance for his influence on Inigo Jones; Vignola, on the other hand, appealed much more strongly, in terms of both temperament and the actual architectural results, to Sir William Chambers.

As well as these great Italian theorists, I have also included Scamozzi, partly from sentiment, because a seventeenth-century English edition of his treatise was one of the earliest parallels to which I had access, and partly as a foil to his predecessors. Vincenzo Scamozzi (1552–1616) published his *L'Idea dell'Architettura Universale* a year before his death. He was a pupil of Palladio, whose influence is apparent throughout his interpretation of the orders. At the same time his contribution was largely academic – he was greatly concerned with harmonies and theories of numbers – but in the event, as the plates show, his orders are of all my examples the most elaborate and enriched. I have added Claude Perrault (1613–88) to stand for the great tradition of French Renaissance thought. Of all the theorists, it was Perrault who refined the whole business of the orders to its most logical and immutable form. Rigidly controlled by a triple system of modules, his orders march inexorably upwards, with column lengths and pedestal heights evenly spaced, but alone among the authorities he keeps the height of his entablatures constant at two diameters throughout, with the effect that his composite column appears much more lofty than any other, far outgrowing the size of its superimposed entablature.

Of English theorists I have chosen two, Gibbs and Chambers. They are quite strongly contrasted. James Gibbs (1682–1754), a student of Wren, in 1732 published a book on the orders which was very different from anything that had appeared before. Apart from its entirely original method of proportioning, it eschewed all reference to origins, mythological or otherwise, and confined itself solely to instructing the reader in the setting out of the orders, their components and their ancillary elements. It thus does not claim to be a philosophical or aesthetic treatise, but simply a practical textbook. It is upon Gibbs's *Rules for Drawing the Several Parts of Architecture* (1732) that this book is chiefly based; it is the closest parallel to the straightforward textbook I have tried to produce, and moreover, it has a place in my affections as the book from which I first copied examples of the orders, and learnt how to set out the volute and the diminution of the column.

My final authority, Sir William Chambers (1723–96), must be admitted to carrying greater intellectual weight. His admirable book *A Treatise on Civil Architecture*, first published under that title in 1759, seems to me to be the most perfect of all the parallels of the orders. In it, Chambers expounds the principles of proportion with a wealth of reference to earlier authorities, all of whom he was fully conversant with. He insists on conformity where it is needed, but allows for a great deal of latitude in the interpretation of the orders and makes no attempt to conceal his own preferences, condemning where he feels condemnation is justified, but always providing as objective reasons as he can for his critical choices. The book is nicely balanced, with historical and mythological references, and whenever we feel Chambers is becoming stuffy or dogmatic he redeems himself with a wry shaft of wit. A fine balance too is maintained between the descriptions of the orders themselves and their employment, and the book is exquisitely illustrated.

These, then, are my chosen mentors – Vitruvius for Rome; Serlio, Vignola, Palladio, Scamozzi for Italy; Perrault for France; and Gibbs and Chambers for England. I first of all prepared a series of mathematical tables, setting out the proportions of the orders as described by each. Plates 4–8 were then drawn primarily from these tables, so that the drawings would wear an evenness of style, although, of course, I made reference to illustrations of the originals from time to time. With the five finished plates before me it was comparatively easy to reach decisions regarding the proportions to be adopted in my own ideal versions of each. I have described this process of selection in the note on plate 9. I hope that my readers will understand the reasons for my choices, even where they dissent from them. Chambers rejected the ideal of absolute, unvarying values for the proportions of the orders – the effect of visible objects, he says, 'is not alone produced by the image on the organ of sight, but by a series of reasoning and association of idea, impressed and guiding the mind in its decision... Perfection consists in mediums between extremes; and forcible effects are produced by verging towards them: all which, the rules of art tend to point out and to explain'.[3] I have endeavoured, in selecting and refining the proportions of my five orders, to follow Chambers's advice and choose always the middle course between extremes.

TRADITIONAL SYSTEMS OF PROPORTION

Apart from some ambiguities, Vitruvius sets out the proportions of the orders with considerable precision. The principle is established in his writing of taking the diameter of the column at its base as the unit of measurement. The proportions of the various elements of the order are derived from this unit, albeit not always directly, as a series of fractions.

3. Sir William Chambers, *A Treatise on the Decorative Part of Civil Architecture*, pp. 107–8.

For example, the height of the Ionic architrave (depending on the column height) may be expressed as half the base diameter, but further dimensions of the entablature are given as fractions of the architrave dimension rather than the column base. This breakdown into fractions of fractions leads to some very awkward figures; for instance, the dimension of one and a half eighteenths of the base diameter is prescribed for the recession of the volute behind the face of the abacus, in the same order.[4] Alberti largely forsook this somewhat ad hoc progress of measurement in favour of a more rational system. The basic unit is the semi-diameter of the column at its base. This is divided into 30 minutes, so that with a 5/6 diminution of the shaft the column diameters are expressed as 60 minutes and 50 minutes at the base and head respectively. While some of the major elements and their principal subdivisions may be described in simple fractions of the diameter or semi-diameter, all the smaller subdivisions are given in terms of thirtieths of the module.

This system of proportions was enthusiastically adopted by almost all subsequent Renaissance writers, though some preferred to regard the full diameter rather than the semi-diameter as the fundamental unit – a somewhat academic distinction as described by Palladio: 'The module shall be the diameter of the column at the bottom, divided into sixty minutes; except in the Doric order, where the module is but half the diameter of the column, divided into thirty minutes, because it is thus more commodious in the divisions of the said order'[5] – and even further complicated by Perrault, who insisted upon a Great module, equal to the diameter, of 60 minutes, a Mean module of 30 and a Little module of 20 minutes.

It was not until the publication of James Gibbs's *Rules for Drawing the Several Parts of Architecture* in 1732 that this modular system was challenged. Gibbs claimed to have perfected 'a more exact and easy manner than has been heretofore practised, by which all fractions, in dividing the principal members and their parts, are avoided'.[6] In his introduction he summarises the traditional system of modular proportions and points out the danger of mistakes in a system of modules, minutes and seconds, as well as criticising 'the difficulty of dividing those small points with Compasses'. Gibbs's system in a sense represents a return to the Vitruvian method of fractions of fractions. Each order demands a multiple scale. The whole height of the order is divided into five equal parts, one being apportioned to the pedestal and four to column and entablature. Column and entablature are divided (4:1 in Tuscan and Doric, 5:1 in the remainder), the entablatures are divided into equal parts depending on the order, and the components of the order again divided. Although Gibbs avoids the apparent awkwardness of some Vitruvian fractions, his system is again one of compound subdivision. It suffers from a tendency for the proportions of individual components to be viewed separately, rather than as components of an orderly whole.

Gibbs's doubts about the accuracy of marking out small fractions with 'the compasses' is interesting as it reminds us that the dividers, now seldom seen beside a drawing board, were until quite recently an essential item of equipment. The use of set scales for drawing is quite a recent innovation. Although every Renaissance draftsman would use a full-size

4. Vitruvius, *The Ten Books on Architecture*, Book 3, Chapter 5.

5. Palladio, *The Four Books of Architecture*, Book 1, Chapter 13.

6. James Gibbs, *Rules for Drawing the Several Parts of Architecture*. Note on the title page.

scale of feet and inches, set scales of so many feet to the inch were unknown. The scale of a particular drawing was determined by the size of the building to be depicted and the size of the piece of paper on which it was to be drawn. A scale unique to that drawing would be prepared using what was known as a sector, a pair of scales joined at one end by a pivot, so one could be set at a chosen angle to another, and the particular scale required produced from one of a series of standard scales engraved upon them. My English edition of Scamozzi, dating from 1637, for example, includes a lengthy description of a sector or Joint-Rule as it is called, together with a drawing. It is claimed to enable the user, among other things, to determine 'the lengths and angles of rafters, hips and collar beams in any square or bevelling roofs at any pitch', but its primary purpose was for setting out scales of 30 or 60 minutes to one module. Draftsmen were proficient in transferring dimensions to drawings from individually prepared scales by means of dividers, a skill which has lapsed comparatively recently.

A METRIC SYSTEM OF MEASUREMENT

Two recent innovations have, I suggest, dramatically changed the way in which we go about the business of preparing scale drawings. One is the change to the metric system, the other the introduction of the pocket calculator. A duodecimal system of feet and inches allowed for a number of permutations of division into fractions, but was not amenable to division by ten. A metric system of measurement by definition is a system geared to decimal fractions rather than thirds, halves and quarters. The difficulties of computing fractions disappear with the use of the pocket calculator, which is not aware that one half is an easier figure to contemplate than one and a half eighteenths. It occurred to me, therefore, as soon as I began to compile the setting out of the comparative orders of various authorities, that the use of a decimal system for describing the proportions of the orders would circumvent a great deal of tedious arithmetic, and produce a system of proportions readily understood and easy to adapt to any size in practice.

All the proportions set out in the accompanying plates are therefore given in *decimal fractions of the diameter of the column at its base*. Only three instances occurred where this system caused any difficulty whatsoever. They all concern components whose proportions or spacing are measured in thirds or fractions of thirds of the column diameter. One is the triglyph of the Doric order, the second the spacing of Corinthian and Composite modillions and consoles, and the third the dimension of the splayed corner of the abacus in the more complex orders. The dimensions given in the relevant plates show how these problems have been resolved.

Considerable thought was given to organising the plates in the most helpful manner, bearing in mind the function of the book as a practical manual. In setting out any order, it is likely that the designer will start by knowing, with some degree of accuracy, the overall height within which it is to be contained, and with less certainty the possible range of column spacings. The first essential is therefore to be able to select readily the leading proportions, namely the height of column, entablature and pedestal. The possibility was first examined of making the overall height of each order one unit and expressing all the parts as decimal fractions of this, but this was rejected for two reasons. First, some very small and cumbersome figures resulted, though this could have been alleviated by calling the height 100 or 1,000 rather than one. More important, the overall height in practice depends on a number of choices: whether or not the principal order is to stand on a pedestal, whether orders are to be superimposed, whether attics, blocking courses and basements are to be incorporated and so forth. In any case, some affinity with traditional methods of proportioning was felt to be desirable, so a decimal scale based on the column diameter was decided upon as the most practical method of indicating proportions.

The scales attached to each plate require some explanation. To begin with plate 9 – the five orders (p. 55). The left and right margins of this plate contain graphical scales graduated in whole column diameters. It will be seen that these scales commence at zero at the underside of the square plinth of the column base, rising through the column and entablature, and falling through the pedestal. This is because the pedestal seems to be the element most likely to be omitted from the order in use. To the right of each order is a further figured scale indicating for each the overall height of pedestal, column and entablature. Plate 9 is intended to serve as a handy comparative reference or index to the orders, and might be used, for example, when making an initial choice of the order to be employed in particular circumstances.

Each of the subsequent plates showing an order in full, for example plate 10, the Tuscan order, has four scales down its left hand margin, as in Fig. 1.

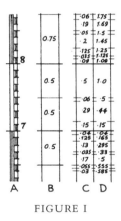

FIGURE I

Scale A is a repetition of the graphical scales of plate 9, ascending and descending from the underside of the column plinth, but further subdivided into tenths of the column diameter. Adjacent to it figured scale B shows the proportions of the principal divisions and subdivisions of the order. It is intended that it should be possible to draw the outline of the order from the information given in these two scales. The left hand part of each of the drawings of the orders in full is devoted to a kind of skeleton of the order, showing the main construction lines, which will enable the draftsman to set out the order quite rapidly, without having to worry with the complexities of individual mouldings and so forth. (Nothing is new, of course; no sooner had I determined my 'skeleton' orders than I received a new facsimile reprint of Batty Langley's *The Builder's Jewel* in which the orders are set out in the same simplified fashion.[7])

7. Batty Langley, *The Builder's Jewel*, plate 1 et seq.

Two additional figured scales C and D are provided. Scale C shows the proportions of the minor subdivisions, and scale D repeats these in running or cumulative figures. One of the chief exasperations of setting out detail dimensions is that especially when drawing to a small scale it is difficult for even the most meticulous draftsman to make a whole series of fractions, separately measured, add up to the correct total. The use of a running scale obviates this difficulty. It will be noted that two zero-points are taken for scales C and D, the bottom of the column plinth and the bottom of the entablature. It is easiest when setting out to establish these principal points first, and then work from them. Besides, it will often be necessary to draw the entablature without the column. In the plates devoted to details, some of these scales are sometimes omitted, but the purpose of the scales employed should be sufficiently clear in each case.

Horizontal proportions are similarly given as individual and running dimensions in most cases. Here, there occurs what may be thought to be an inconsistency. In the plates of the full orders, horizontal proportions are always figured from the centre-line of the column, but in the detail plates of the entablatures (e.g. plate 11) they are figured from the face of the frieze. Again, this is because of the frequent requirement to draw entablature without column, as in the design of a cornice surmounting a plain wall. It should always be clear from the plate which kind of scale is being used; what is important to remember is the horizontal dimension from column centre-line to face of frieze, which is 0.425 rather than 0.5, owing to the diminution in column diameter from base to head.

It is suggested that it is considerably easier to set out the orders from these decimal scales than from the modular system contained in previous parallels. Once the order to be employed has been selected, and its overall height established, the base diameter can readily be determined, either by calculation or by drawing an inclined scale along the lines described elsewhere.[8] If the base diameter is found by calculation, it can be entered in the memory of a pocket calculator, and multiplied with each of the figured proportions given to determine the actual size of each subdivision of the order. Removing the tedium of proportioning the subdivisions reduces errors and leaves the draftsman free to concentrate on the business of design.

The table below sets out the decimal equivalents of the sixty parts of the module or column diameter, and may be of assistance to those who wish to transcribe direct from, say, Chambers or Palladio.

	1	2	3	4	5	6	7	8	9	10
0	0.02	0.03	0.05	0.07	0.08	0.1	0.12	0.13	0.15	0.17
10	0.18	0.2	0.22	0.23	0.25	0.27	0.28	0.3	0.32	0.33
20	0.35	0.37	0.38	0.4	0.42	0.43	0.45	0.47	0.48	0.5
30	0.52	0.53	0.55	0.57	0.58	0.6	0.62	0.63	0.65	0.67
40	0.68	0.7	0.72	0.73	0.75	0.77	0.78	0.8	0.82	0.83
50	0.85	0.87	0.88	0.9	0.92	0.93	0.95	0.97	0.98	1

8. Chitham, op. cit., p. 44.

HISTORICAL BACKGROUND

THE GREEK ORDERS: DORIC, IONIC AND CORINTHIAN

The starting point for any study of the orders is Ancient Greece. The great succession of Renaissance writers who regularised the orders more or less ignored Greece, partly because of its comparative inaccessibility, although Vitruvius had been in no doubt, to judge from the references to Greek architecture which articulate his treatise, of the significance of the Greek origins of Roman architectural form. It was not until after the middle of the eighteenth century, with the explorations of such Western visitors as The Society of Dilettante, and in particular the commencement of *The Antiquities of Athens* by Stuart and Revett, that notice began to be taken of Greek precedents.

As knowledge of Ancient Greece became consolidated, arguments between the pro-Grecians and the pro-Romans proliferated, and these arguments lasted up to and beyond the general lapse in interest in classical architecture. Indeed, the view that the Greeks were a race of pure aesthetes whose architecture reached a summit of perfection and the Romans simply a brutish race of copyists, lacking in intellect and inventiveness, was still current in my schooldays.

Clearly the truth is not such a stark matter of sheep and goats. Rome achieved a political importance and social complexity far beyond anything the Greeks dreamed of, and the development of Roman architecture and engineering reflects this complexity. Whilst the intellectual sophistication of the Greeks reached an astonishing level, the organisation and scale of their society was restricted by comparison, and this is reflected in the limited range of buildings to which their architectural skills were addressed.

Nor is Greece the original source of the classical orders, but rather the place in which they came first to maturity. Capitals of Doric form appear in earlier civilisations – the idea of spreading a beam load by a broad pad on top of a post must be almost as old as posts and beams themselves – and are practically universal in Cretan and Minoan work. Volutes and flower-decoration, the progenitors of the Ionic capital, are common in ancient architecture of the Near East, and fluting and moulded entablatures appear in Egypt. The Greeks brought together many strands of architectural thought and over a period from about 700 B.C. onwards evolved the orders, recognisable and classifiable in all their elements.

More particularly, they evolved the Doric and the Ionic. There is a tendency to regard the Doric order, I suppose because it is the simplest, as the earliest of the five orders, and the Ionic as a later and more sophisticated development. In fact, these two orders developed alongside one another, the separation between them being of geography rather than time. Examples of mature Doric style precede the Ionic, but not by very much.

History books tend to oversimplify great racial movements. The Dorians were said to come from the north and drove out the Achaeans (who had earlier overwhelmed the Minoans) and pushed the Ionians to the east, where they occupied the fringe of Asia Minor and the islands of the Aegean. It is hard to believe that there were clear-cut boundaries between their territories, or even that the races were for long distinguishable. It is true, however, that the preponderance of early Doric buildings are located either in the Peloponnese, or more commonly in Sicily and Italy. Compared with the time-scale of evolution in, say, Egyptian architecture, the rate of development of the Doric order was quite rapid. Setting aside Minoan and Achaean proto-Doric, few structures of any advanced level of development occur before 700 B.C. The earliest peripteral Doric temple of note, the Heraeum at Olympia, dates from about 590 B.C. The evidence it provides is somewhat confusing as it was originally constructed entirely of timber, the columns being replaced in stone over a period of centuries. Some of the temples at Selinus and Paestum, only half a century later, exhibit all the characteristics of the whole order.

In the Doric order (plate 1) the fluted *column* rises direct from a raised *stylobate*, without a moulded base, and is terminated by a convex cushion *capital* – the *echinus* – supporting a plain, square *abacus*. The transition between shaft and echinus is marked by a series of horizontal grooves, or by a hollow moulding sometimes embellished with carved leaf-forms, an archaic idiom. The *entablature* has a plain *architrave* surmounted by a narrow *fillet* (*taenia*), the *frieze* of *metopes* either plain or carrying bas-reliefs, separated by grooved *triglyphs* with corresponding tenons (*regulae*) projecting below the taenia and carrying a number of pegs (*guttae*). Above is an oversailing *cornice*, canted on the underside and carrying rectangular blocks (*mutules*) adorned with further rows of guttae. The *corona* of the cornice has a flat fascia crowned by a further moulding, a number of profiles being used, or by decorative *anthemia* etc. (or by both).

The development of the Greek Doric order over the next 200 years is a matter of refinement rather than revolution. As the order developed further from its timber origins and as the builders became more conversant with the techniques of construction in stone, columns became more slender, more liberally spaced, the spread of capitals diminished, proportions and profiles of the mouldings and the elements of the entablature were refined.

Plate 1 shows ((a) and (b)) two column capitals from adjacent temples at Paestum in Italy. The capital of the Basilica (c. 530 B.C.) is of the archaic form with stylised leaf-carvings in the *scotia* separating shaft and capital; that of the temples of Poseidon, some seventy years later, substitutes grooves at the neck of the echinus as well as three further grooves immediately beneath the top of the fluted shaft, a classical configuration, although the spread of the echinus itself is still somewhat broad. Figures (c), (d) and (e) are of the Athenian Treasury at Delphi. This building, constructed just before 500 B.C. is a useful example as it is largely complete and demonstrates all the elements of the order in a very small compass (although it is not of course peripteral like larger temple buildings). Column and capitals are of great elegance of profile, and the capitals of the responding *antae* (d) have reached a classical form. The form of the frieze is complete, with almost exactly square metopes, though presumably because of the small scale of the building there are only five guttae in the regula, and five rows above. The prominence of the flat *fascia* of the cornice, carried up around the pediment, is of note, compared with the insignificance of the *cyma* above. Later on, only the fillet bordering this fascia continues uninterrupted into the

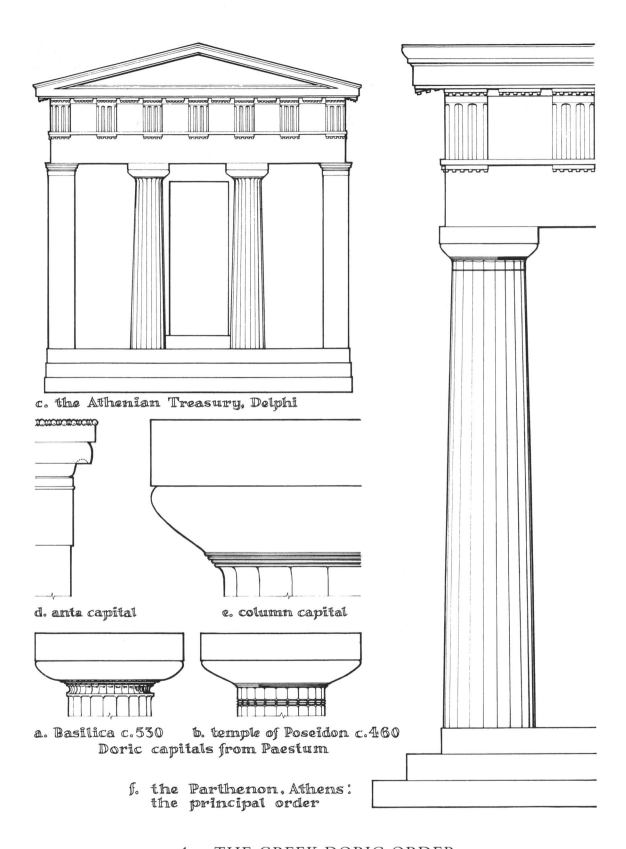

c. the Athenian Treasury, Delphi

d. anta capital   e. column capital

a. Basilica c.530   b. temple of Poseidon c.460
Doric capitals from Paestum

f. the Parthenon, Athens:
   the principal order

1.   THE GREEK DORIC ORDER

31

raking cornice. Figure (f) depicts a corner column from the Parthenon, dating from 447 to 432 B.C., and this may be taken to represent the full flowering of classical Greek Doric. The curve of the echinus is now so tightly controlled that any further restriction would, one feels, cause it to disappear altogether. The fluted shaft (twenty flutes) is curved in an almost imperceptible *entasis*. The use of mouldings in the cornice is very sparing.

It is held that the intense refinement of the Greek Doric order led to its decline. For the designer it contained one overriding limitation which has to do with the form and disposition of the elements of the frieze. As the order evolved, it became the rule that metopes should be square, and that at the corners the two triglyphs on adjoining faces of the frieze should meet. The reconciling of these rules is so restrictive, on both the thickness (front to back) of the architrave and the spacing of columns, that it is most tortuous to resolve. It is interesting, in the two examples in plate 1, to see how the design is affected. In the Athenian Treasury the architrave width is considerably compressed. The corners of the architrave are visibly inset from the line of the antae, compared with the architrave of the Parthenon which oversails the upper diameter of the shaft. In the Parthenon, the problem is resolved by the contraction of the column spacing at the corner, and by accepting an off-centre location for the triglyphs with respect to the column axes.

Roman and Renaissance architects, of course, simply bypassed the problem by accepting that the triglyphs on adjacent faces did not touch at the corner, but were separated by a sliver of metope. Greek sensitivity allowed for no such evasion. Thus the Greek Doric order may be compared with a species of animal evolved to a state of limited perfection and then doomed to extinction.

The Ionic order (plate 2) is subject to no such trammels. Indeed, apart from the Tuscan, not represented in Greek architecture, it is the most tractable of all the orders in terms of column spacing and the negotiation of corners. This is because there are no large scale elements in the enrichment of its entablature: the close but flexible rhythm of the dentils imposes no dimensional restrictions.

There are two ways of regarding the capital which gives the order its most readily identifiable characteristic. Although many examples of proto-Ionic are simply plant forms developed on the drum of the column, some early prototypes, such as that from Neandria, exhibit *volutes* on front and rear faces only, with a corresponding roll or cushion-shape to the sides. The alternative form is based on volutes drawn out symmetrically on the axes of the diagonals of the abacus. This type is much rarer in Greece, although the Ionic capitals at Bassae are outstanding examples. (See also the notes on plates 20 and 21.)

The chief characteristics of the classical Ionic order are represented in plate 2 by two examples, the order from the temple on the Ilissus at Athens, c. 450 B.C. (a) and the entablature of the temple of Athena Polias at Priene (b), a much later example of c. 335 B.C. The first of these two shows the essential elements of the column. It rises from an elaborate base of two *torus* mouldings separated by a shallow *scotia*, the upper torus horizontally fluted. The column is slightly more than eight diameters in height, fluted with twenty-four flutes separated by fillets, and terminated in a directional voluted capital supporting a plain *ovolo*-edged abacus. The volutes of the capital oversail an enriched ovolo over an astragal; in the case of the column depicted, the corner is nicely turned by drawing out the angle volute on the diagonal, hinting at the alternative multi-directional capital.

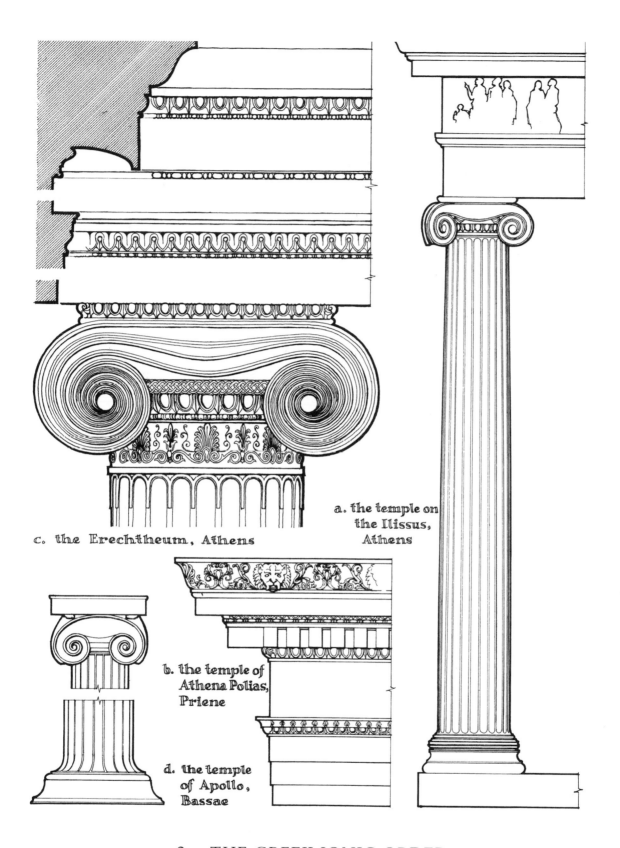

c. the Erechtheum, Athens

a. the temple on the Ilissus, Athens

b. the temple of Athena Polias, Priene

d. the temple of Apollo, Bassae

2. THE GREEK IONIC ORDER

The entablature of the Ilissus temple is uncharacteristically plain, although it has a sculptured continuous frieze. The entablature of Athena Polias is a fully evolved Ionic type which stands as the norm for the order. The frieze is divided into three stepped faces and surmounted by a composite *cavetto-over-ovolo* moulding. The frieze is a continuous flat band, and the cornice includes a *dentil* course beneath the corona, and a bold crowning cyma.

Figure (c) shows details of the order from the north porch of the Erechtheum at Athens. Dating from the end of the fifth century B.C. this sumptuous building exhibits to a supreme degree the elaboration to which the Ionic order might be taken, and poses a striking contrast to the stern restraint of contemporary Doric work. The capital, its abacus embellished with egg and dart, has volutes with multiple spiral bands, and beneath the astragal an added band of *lotus* and *palmette* in bas-relief. Mouldings in the architrave and cornice are profusely enriched, the frieze a continuous sculpture of white marble figures on a black Eleusian stone background.

Figure (d) is of the internal order of the temple of Apollo at Bassae, and is taken from Cockerell's restoration. Dating from about 420 B.C., this temple is curious in that all three orders are represented in it. The peripteral order is a conventional Doric, but internally it contains this Ionic order with massive bell-like bases and the volutes tightly spaced, connected with a pleasing humped curve under a solid square abacus. Moreover, a single axial column terminating the internal vista has a capital which is clearly of Corinthian (or Composite) form.

The Corinthian order (plate 3) makes only a fleeting and tentative appearance in the architecture of classical Greece. The solitary Corinthian column within the temple of Apollo Epicurius (a) is an extraordinary, isolated example. It has two rows of *acanthus*, diminutive in scale, eight pairs of voluted *calyces* and a concave-sided abacus, all the principal components of the Corinthian capital, albeit in rudimentary form. Only the column itself is identifiably Corinthian – the entablature is shared with the adjacent Ionic columns.

Likewise, in the Choragic Monument of Lysicrates (b), built nearly 100 years later in 334 B.C., innovation is confined to the column, the entablature with its crowning *acroteria* being purely Ionic. The form is again highly individual, with a miniature row of acanthus and a second row much larger in scale, then extravagantly voluted calyces. For the first time a palmette appears in the centre of the abacus, which is shaped with ovolo above scotia. The column flutings terminate in leaf mouldings.

Contemporary with this is the capital from the Tholos at Epidaurus (c). This capital is of conventional Corinthian form, the two tiers of acanthus and the surmounting volutes fully developed and delicately carved, the underlying bell clearly expressed. The two final examples are really from the post-Hellenic period. First, a capital from the Tower of the Winds at Athens (d) dating from 170 B.C. with a single tier of acanthus, and plain waterleaves clasping the upper part of the bell and supporting a moulded square abacus. Lastly, a Graeco-Roman example from the late Olympieum at Athens (e), rebuilt over a long period between 170 B.C. and A.D. 130. Apart from the diminished proportion of the volutes, this is practically the Corinthian capital of Roman and Renaissance architecture.

a. the temple of Apollo,
Bassae

b. the choragic
monument of
Lysicrates, Athens

c. capital from the Tholos,
Epidaurus

d. the Tower
of the Winds,
Athens

e.
the Olympieum
Athens

3.   THE GREEK CORINTHIAN ORDER

35

PLATE 4

COMPARATIVE TUSCAN ORDERS

Vitruvius divorces his discussion of the Tuscan order from that of the other orders, treating it in a somewhat more antiquarian manner. He describes the Tuscan temple as a whole before going on to an account of the order itself. A full description is given of the column with its base and capital, but the entablature is described in structural terms and its proportions dealt with in broad terms only.[9]

For this reason Vitruvius has been omitted from this plate, which begins with Serlio. Serlio acknowledges Vitruvius's establishment of the column height as 7 diameters. However, he goes on to quote his contention that the Doric order originally had a column 6 diameters in height, in imitation of the proportions of the human body. Remarking that Vitruvius then settles for 7 diameters as the proper proportion for the Doric, he argues that the simpler Tuscan ought to be shorter.[10] Thus he arrives at a proportion of 6 diameters, which gives a very stocky appearance and, as the plate indicates, proves too squat a proportion to commend itself to any subsequent authority. Serlio's entablature is of the simplest, the cornice having a bold corona surmounted by an ovolo and supported by a simple fillet, oddly reminiscent of Greek prototypes. He allows the pedestal proportions to vary according to the location and purpose of the order.

Both Serlio and Vignola follow Vitruvius in proposing a circular plinth for the Tuscan, a curious form presumably intended to emphasise the archaic and somewhat rustic nature of the order, as if the columns were erected upon millstones. In other respects, Vignola's is a transitional interpretation, setting a column height of 7 diameters which is subsequently followed by Palladio and Gibbs, but only embellishing the cornice a little more than Serlio. Scamozzi envisages a column height of 7½ diameters, and Perrault 7⅓, but whereas Perrault provides a variation on the cornice suggested by Serlio and Vignola, Scamozzi shows an elaborate cornice with cyma and fillets above and ovolo and a further cyma below the corona. Furthermore, he suggests a kind of blank triglyph in the frieze over the capital (though not in the beam between columns) as well as an architrave split into two faces.

The standard for the order is set, perhaps, by Palladio. His frieze and architrave are unadorned and the abacus of the column a plain block. The cornice has a boldly moulded *cyma* above the corona, and below a *cavetto* surmounted by a cyma flowing into the soffit of the corona to form a weathering. Gibbs does not really improve on this. His cornice mouldings are similar, though with a simple ovolo over the lower cavetto – a mirror of the

---

9. Vitruvius, *op. cit.*, Book 4, Chapter 7.
10. Serlio, *The Five Books of Architecture*, Book 4, Chapter 5.

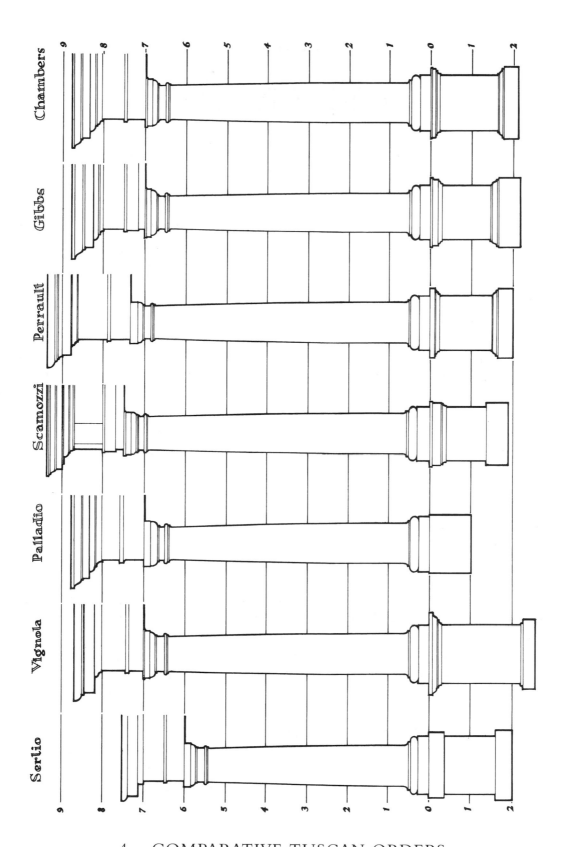

4. COMPARATIVE TUSCAN ORDERS

37

'box cornices' of countless early eighteenth-century English houses – and he cannot resist subdividing the architrave, and adding a small fillet to the upper edge of the abacus, as proposed by Scamozzi. Chambers in general follows Vignola, but rejects his cornice as 'far inferior to the rest of the composition' and substitutes 'that of Scamozzi, with such alterations as were evidently necessary to render it perfect'.[11] The pedestal of his order is refined from that of Vignola.

The Tuscan is the only order in which the fillet that terminates the shaft above the torus of the base is included within the half-diameter dimension of the base itself. This is presumably because the simplicity of form of the Tuscan base permits all its three components to be embraced within a semi-diameter without crowding. Chambers takes Scamozzi to task for excluding this fillet. As the plate shows, Scamozzi's plinth is unduly high and coarse in proportion as a result of this practice, of which he appears to be the only exponent.

11. Chambers, *op. cit.*, pp. 42–3.

PLATE 5

COMPARATIVE DORIC ORDERS

Vitruvius sets the general pattern for the capital and entablature of the Doric order. He starts with a consideration of the problems of the arrangement of triglyphs and metopes which I have already cited as stifling the development of the Greek Doric order. It appears that early Doric work of the republican era in Rome followed Greek precedent in the layout of the frieze, the temple at Cori dating from the first century B.C. being an example. By the time of Vitruvius Roman architects had learnt to short-circuit the problem by simply aligning the triglyphs centrally over their columns, and allowing a part-metope at the corners of the frieze. This practice Vitruvius endorses and describes in considerable detail, down to the profile of the vertical grooves in the triglyphs 'cut to fit the tip of a carpenter's square'.[12]

In two respects, the proportions he establishes are not followed by Renaissance writers. First, he restricts the column height to 7 diameters, producing a rather bulky form, and second, presumably following Greek practice, he offers no dimensions for a moulded base, so that the Vitruvian column rises abruptly from the stylobate. A peculiarity of the Greek Doric adopted by Vitruvius is the downward slope of the soffit of the corona, subsequently dismissed by Chambers as producing an unstable appearance.

Serlio discusses the absence of bases from Vitruvian Doric at some length and concludes that the *Attic base* to which Vitruvius refers is the proper base for the Doric.

This base, which with some embellishment applies also to the Ionic, Corinthian and Composite orders, incorporates two tori separated by a scotia. Serlio also illustrates an alternative form, in which *astragals* are introduced between the tori, termed by Vitruvius an *Ionic base*. He adopts the height of 7 diameters for the column, but criticises the lack of projection of Vitruvius's capital. He shows various alternative capitals including some with three fillets stepping out beneath the echinus, which may be enriched, and one with rosettes in the neck. He includes vigorous drawings of bosses and *bucranian* masks adorning the metopes of the frieze, and diamond shaped and other panel enrichments between the mutules. The plate shows one of a variety of Serlio's entablatures in which the mutules are either omitted in favour of a panelled soffit to the corona, or concealed behind its projecting face.

Vignola prefers a column height of 8 diameters and alternates rosettes with husks in the neck of the column. He and all subsequent authorities show the Attic base, and he establishes the proportions and mouldings of the entablature followed, with minor variations,

---

12. Vitruvius, OP. CIT., Book 4, Chapter 3.

by Gibbs and Chambers. In this order Perrault's column and entablature heights agree for once with the majority, but his cornice is enriched by additional mouldings above the corona. Both Palladio and Scamozzi exceed the generally accepted height with column heights of 8⅔ and 8½ diameters respectively. Palladio's capital and base are largely conventional, but he introduces to this and his subsequent bases a curious concave weathering which merges the plinth into the upper part of the pedestal cornice. Both Palladio and Scamozzi divide the frieze into two faces, and Scamozzi interposes a dentil band in the cornice to produce the tallest of any Doric entablature with a somewhat hybrid appearance.

Chambers' Doric is generally similar to that of Vignola and has been omitted from the plate. He makes some interesting points in his accompanying notes, however, in particular concerning the limitation on column spacings imposed by the rhythm of metope and triglyph (see plate 36) and the awkwardness of the mutular form of cornice. Chambers allows for some deviation in the height of the Doric column according to its location.[13]

13. Chambers, *op. cit.*, p. 52.

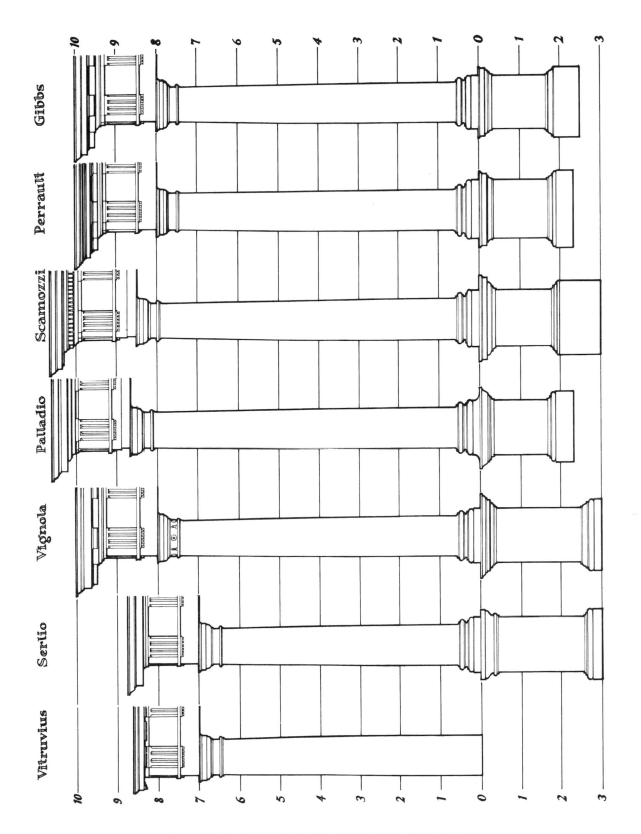

5. COMPARATIVE DORIC ORDERS

PLATE 6

COMPARATIVE IONIC ORDERS

As the orders become more complex and more richly embellished, so there is less uniformity in different opinions regarding their composition and proportions. In the consideration of the Ionic order, these variations of interpretation seem to be of sufficient interest to warrant the illustration of examples from all eight of the chosen authorities.

First Vitruvius, whose allocation of 9 diameters to the height of the column meets with the approval of the majority of later authorities (although he cites an 8:1 proportion as used by the ancients). He describes the precise proportions for the capital, but unfortunately his method of setting out the volute forms one of the diagrams appended to his book which have not of course survived. The entablature of the Vitruvian Ionic is again simple and somewhat massive when compared with Renaissance examples, with the architrave in three faces, a frieze of considerable depth and a pronounced dentil course. Not unnaturally, Vitruvius advocates the Ionic base, with its astragals inserted in the scotia for this order, and in this he is imitated by Serlio, Vignola, Palladio and Perrault. Serlio explains succinctly the setting out of the volute. The eye of the volute is divided into six equal parts along its vertical diameter. The volute is composed of a series of semi-circles drawn in succession from these dividing points, the change of radius in each case occurring along the extended diameter, which is termed the *catheta*. The radius of the volute thus diminishes only twice in each revolution, causing considerable distortion and making it appear to lean outwards in an odd manner. Later authors prescribe more sophisticated methods of drawing the volute (see plate 18). It is noticeable that in his freer sketches Serlio himself does not stick rigidly to this form but produces, freehand, more regularly rounded volutes. In other ways, too, Serlio's version is singular. As well as a conventional dentilled form he shows a more elaborate variation, which I have illustrated, with both dentils and consoles, over a *pulvinated* frieze. His column, in accordance with the progression he has worked out for his orders, is restricted to 8 diameters in height.

Vignola's Ionic, adhering to the common 9 diameter column height, adopts an antique form of Ionic base which omits the lower torus. Otherwise it contains all the elements present in the order of the Thermae of Diocletion at Rome (A.D. 306), as is well illustrated by Normand's plates of the two orders,[14] with a prominent dentil course and three faces to the architrave. Vignola's entablature, at 2.25 diameters, is the deepest of any since Vitruvius, and is copied by Chambers who, however, prefers to divide the architrave into two faces only, reserving the division into three for the Corinthian.

14. R. A. Cordingley, *Normand's Parallel of the Orders of Architecture*, plates 28, 33.

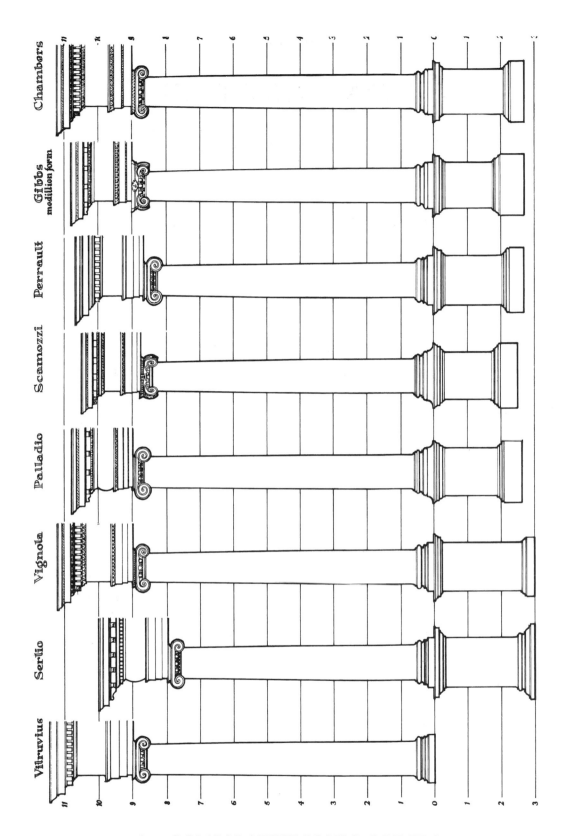

6. COMPARATIVE IONIC ORDERS

Chambers adopts a very similar entablature for his principal illustration of the Ionic, compounded from a number of antique sources. As alternatives he gives two Palladian examples, from the Villa Capra and the Basilica at Vicenza, though he dismisses as low and clumsy the *pulvinated* frieze with which both are furnished. Both have modillions beneath the corona, and indeed Palladio gives no example of the *denticular* form. Gibbs offers both *modillion* and dentil forms – his Ionic seems to be compounded of elements from Scamozzi and Palladio – but like Chambers he shows two faces only to the architrave. Perrault, in the inexorable march of his orders, ascribes a height of 8⅔ diameters to the Ionic.

Scamozzi, whilst following Palladio in most essentials, and imitating his swept plinth, illustrates a capital with the volutes displayed on all four faces, rather than on the front and rear faces only (see also plates 20 and 21). Chambers actually credits Scamozzi with inventing the four-sided volute, or at least improving upon the capitals of the Temple of Concord at Rome (A.D. 10) which have not survived. A kind of prototype exists in Michaelangelo's Palazzo dei Conservatori on the Capitol at Rome, completed about 1545, in which the volutes, although on the front face only, are angled sharply forwards, and their eyes joined by a swag of husks. Moreover, Robertson[15] illustrates a restoration of a four-faced capital from Pompeii, which shows some resemblance to the Bassae order excavated by Cockerell. The popularisation of this type of Ionic capital removes the chief limitation on the use of the order, namely the difficulty of handling the corners, and the four-faced capital is subsequently usually employed except where in neo-classical architecture the designer reverts deliberately to Greek prototypes.

15. D. S. Robertson, *A Handbook of Greek and Roman Architecture*, plate 9.

PLATE 7

COMPARATIVE CORINTHIAN ORDERS

Vitruvius states that the Corinthian and Ionic orders are in all respects alike except for their capitals. Because of the increased depth of the Corinthian capital, he allows a height of 9½ diameters for the column; I have repeated the entablature that he prescribes for the Ionic, with its comparatively simple cornice adorned with a dentil course. Serlio, because he only allows 9 diameters for the column, produces a Corinthian somewhat lacking in the elegance we expect in this order. Moreover, he adopts the capital depth advocated by Vitruvius of 1 diameter only, so that both shaft and capital appear a little stunted. He illustrates the Ionic base for this order, and both denticular and modillioned forms of the entablature, the latter not dissimilar to his modillioned Ionic.

The stateliest Corinthian is that of Vignola, with a column height of 10 diameters and an entablature of 2.5. Chambers clearly regards the Corinthian as the highest in rank of all the orders, placing it last in his hierarchical sequence (as does Scamozzi), so it is perhaps unkind not to afford space in this plate to the version of Chambers. However, he himself admits that his version is based closely on that of Vignola, both being derived primarily from the Temple of Mars Ultor (2 B.C.) and the interior order of the Pantheon. Vignola employs an Ionic base, which Chambers finds gives a wearisome repetition of convex forms, preferring a simple base very similar to that employed in his Doric order. Vignola regularises the capital height at 1⅙ diameters, a proportion subsequently universally adopted which gives space for the proper development of the surrounding leaves (which Chambers says should be modelled on the olive) and of the calyces which spring from them. Vignola introduces both dentils and consoles into his cornice, a practice condemned by Serlio on the authority of Vitruvius, on the somewhat pedantic grounds of confusing two separate forms of roof-construction which these two elements symbolically represent.

In Palladio's version, the column is only allowed a height of 9½ diameters. Both dentils and consoles are again prescribed for the entablature, though curiously, in both his general plates of the order, the dentils are omitted, leaving a plain band between the ovolo and cyma reversa of the lower part of the cornice – perhaps an error on the part of the engraver. Strange things can happen to an architect's drawings en route to publication, as is shown by some of Serlio's columns appearing upside down! For reasons not entirely clear, Chambers is very disparaging about Palladio's Corinthian, accusing him of departing radically from his own rendering of the Mars Ultor (Jupiter Stator) order in Book IV. We may, on the other hand, find such criticism unduly severe, particularly when we inspect the coolly elegant Corinthian orders realised by Palladio, such as that at S. Georgio Maggiore

(1560) in Venice, where he displays to advantage his preference for leaving the leafwork of the capitals simply modelled and pleasantly understated.

Scamozzi follows much of the precedent of his tutor in this order, but prefers the more common column height of 10 diameters. He omits the dentils from the cornice, perhaps on Serlio's advice, but allows both ovolo and cyma reversa below the band of consoles, both enriched, while Perrault, over a column 9⅔ diameters high, employs a cornice in which a plain band is substituted for the dentil course. Gibbs's Corinthian takes its cue from Vignola, but because of his insistence on an entablature : column ratio of 1:5, his cornice, with the elements of Vignola's all repeated, seems a little cramped and crowded.

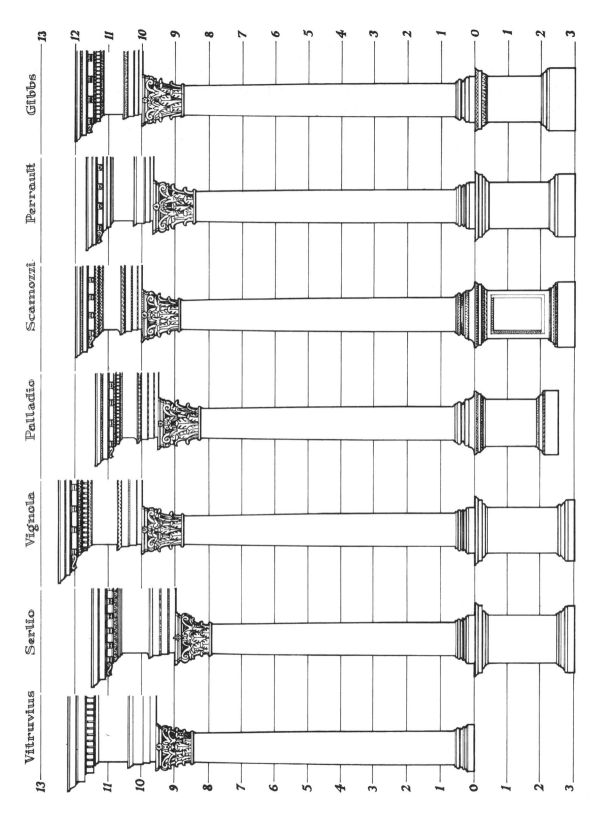

7.   COMPARATIVE CORINTHIAN ORDERS

PLATE 8

COMPARATIVE COMPOSITE ORDERS

The Composite order is a more artificial invention of Renaissance writers than the other four. Many Roman Corinthian versions exhibit what might be termed proto-composite characteristics, especially in the treatment of the capital, but it does not emerge as a separate order in Roman architecture, and it is unknown to Vitruvius.

Indeed, as Mark Wilson Jones has pointed out, Roman architects show considerable pragmatism both in the way their orders are proportioned and in mixing elements from different orders, but the overall arithmetical control they exert over proportions makes it clear that this flexibility is deliberate and by no means illiterate.[16]

Serlio's pioneering version is frankly idiosyncratic. He derives the entablature from the uppermost superimposed external order of the Colosseum, merging frieze into cornice with a series of massive curved brackets set in the frieze and supporting the corona. He also illustrates details of some particularly ebullient capitals and bases including one of Roman origin in which winged horses are substituted for the volutes. The logical progression of his orders permits him to allot a height of 10 diameters to the column, with which all subsequent authorities concur except Scamozzi who prefers 9¾ diameters for his 'Roman' order, in order to emphasise the view, which he shares with Chambers, of its inferiority to the Corinthian.

Vignola offers alternative forms for the Composite entablature. As well as the somewhat pedestrian denticular version shown in the plate, he evolves from Serlio's bracketed entablature a much more graceful bracket which contains clear references to the Doric, both in the vertical grooving with which it is adorned and with the spacing, which leaves square metopes in the frieze to be enriched with bas-reliefs. Summerson has pointed out how this particular idiom caught the imagination of nineteenth-century English classicists.[17]

Despite his reservations, Chambers produces a handsome version of the order, claiming the capital as purely his own interpretation and deriving the proportions of the entablature from both Tuscan and Ionic examples. For the architrave he borrows from Vignola, giving it only two faces separated by an enriched cyma reversa, as indeed do most authors, whilst the cornice, derived from Scamozzi, follows the Corinthian, but with square modillions substituted for the curved consoles. The order of Palladio, and its derivatives by Gibbs, Perrault and Scamozzi, all again suffer from lack of height in the entablature, each being only 2 diameters in height. All have square modillions in the cornice; Scamozzi acknowledges the Ionic ancestry of the order in his triple-faced architrave. Perrault works out the logic of the mathematical progression of his orders, arriving at a column height of 10 diameters, his loftiest order.

16. Mark Wilson Jones, *Principles of Roman Architecture*, pp. 109 et seq.

17. Summerson, *op. cit.*

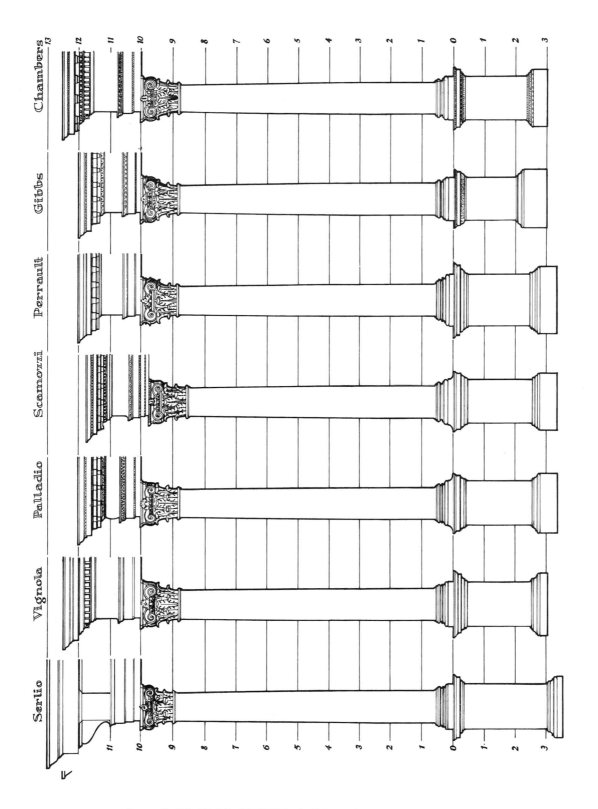

8.   COMPARATIVE COMPOSITE ORDERS

49

THE ORDERS
IN DETAIL

PLATE 9

THE FIVE ORDERS

This plate represents my own distillation of the contents of the preceding plates comparing the orders by different authorities. First, an observation may be made about the manner in which it is set out. In preparing a drawing of this kind, two options are available: either the base diameter of each order can be kept constant, giving a stepped overall height, or the overall height of all the orders can be kept the same and a different module chosen for each. Renaissance writers are divided about this. Chambers is adamant in his opposition to making the module dimension constant: 'To render the comparison between the orders more easy, I have represented them all of the same height; by which means the gradual increase of delicacy and richness is easily perceivable…the proportions of the orders were by the ancients formed on those of the human body and consequently it could not be their intention to make a Corinthian column as thick and much taller than a Doric one.' He goes on to condemn a number of authorities, including Vignola, Scamozzi, Blondel and Perrault, for ascribing an ascending order of height to their orders.

Chambers' reasoning seems to be unacceptable; the comparison with the human body is a tenuous one, and we are seldom likely to use the orders to a human scale. I instinctively regard the orders as having a hierarchy of height, rather than of thickness. Besides, the advantage of setting them out to a common scale for the purposes of this plate needs no defence, as it is intended that the modular height of each will be grasped at a glance, by comparison with its fellows.

The actual proportions I determined upon as a result of comparing the ideal orders of the various Renaissance authorities stem from a number of factors. First, I accept the convention that the orders together form a kind of mathematical progression, from the Tuscan upwards, the column height increasing in steps of one diameter. I am not sufficiently bold to follow Perrault's logical conclusion of this progression and make the Composite taller than the Corinthian. In order to do this, one either has to make the Composite 11 diameters in height, producing an unacceptably attenuated appearance, cut the Tuscan back to Serlio's 6 diameters, or make the steps between successive orders less than 1 diameter as Perrault did. On the other hand, once the Composite is accepted as a variant of the Corinthian in terms of its proportions, the progression of column heights becomes very natural.

Second, I accept that the ratio of entablature to column height should be constant throughout the orders of my metric series. Not all authorities accept this. Gibbs, for example, adopts a ratio of 0.25:1 for Tuscan and Doric and 0.2:1 for the remainder, in broad correspondence with Palladio who, however, has idiosyncratic ideas about the column heights. Chambers follows Vignola in adopting a common ratio of 0.25:1, and it is this that I have followed on the grounds that it allows sufficient stature to the shaft without cramping the proportions of the mouldings of the entablature.

Having adopted a common ratio for the heights of the entablature and column, it seems logical to do the same for the pedestal which, perhaps because of its optional nature, has received much less attention in the past than the remainder of the vocabulary. Gibbs gives to the pedestal one fifth of the total height of the order, Vignola one third. Vignola's pedestals seem uncomfortably lofty; I have opted for a pedestal:column ratio of 0.3:1 throughout. I have been careful to apportion the pedestal height in a progressive way between its components of cornice, die and plinth so that as the die and plinth become more elongated with each successive order, at the same time the height given to cornice and plinth mouldings is increased to accommodate their greater complexity.

With the principal proportions now settled, the design of each order revolves about the selection of individual members either as a result of a general consensus between authorities, or in some cases merely through personal preference. Hence I have discarded devices which appear in only one set of orders, such as Serlio's gigantic bracketed Composite entablature, and similarly the modillion form of the Ionic published by Gibbs as an alternative form. I have followed Chambers' championship of the Corinthian as the culmination of the series, and afforded to it the most delicate and elaborate architrave, as well as reserving to it the curved form of the *consoles* supporting the corona, employing the much more robust square modillions in the cornice of the Composite. The Composite also is the only order to which I have allotted a pulvinated frieze, though a flat frieze would in fact serve here as a perfectly satisfactory alternative. I must express a preference, in the Ionic, for the symmetrical four-sided capital, which seems to me more shapely than its flat-sided counterpart. I have adhered throughout to the Attic base in preference to the Ionic, endorsing Chambers' contention that confusion is occasioned by joining several convex members together.

Beyond these general guidelines, the precise choice of mouldings and the sequence in which they are assembled must be left to the individual. It is the great strength of the orders that within a clear framework of leading proportions they offer scope for a wide variety of individual treatment.

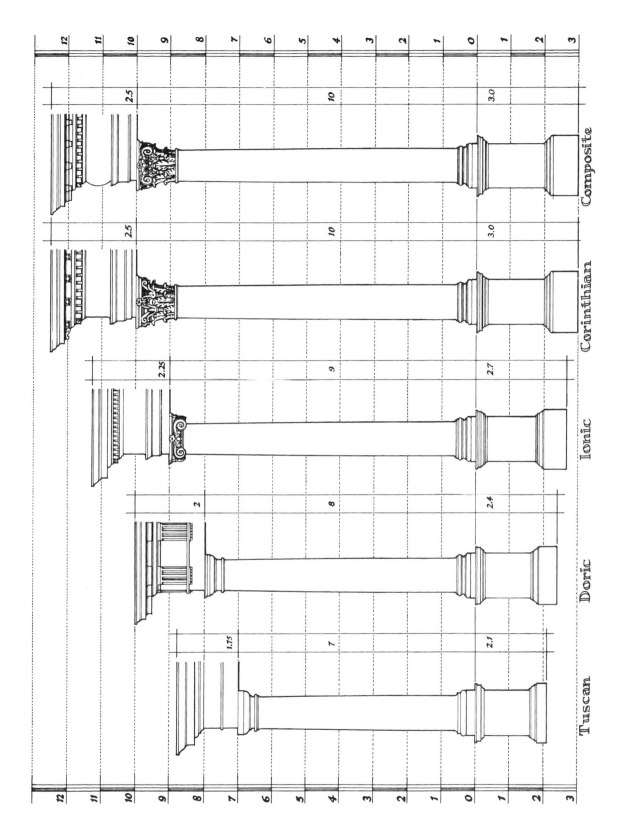

9. THE FIVE ORDERS

PLATE 10

THE TUSCAN ORDER

Figure (a) shows how the Tuscan order may be set out. I have adopted a column height of 7 diameters, with an entablature of 1.75 and a plinth of 2.1. 0.5 is given to the base and 0.5 to the capital, which projects to a total of c.625 from the centre line, rather more than advocated by early authorities such as Serlio, who envisaged the extremity of the abacus as aligning with the base diameter. In accordance with the sequence of dimensions I have worked out for the pedestals of the orders, the die of the Tuscan pedestal is fractionally over-square, being 1.4 wide × 1.35 high.

Figure (b) shows the complete order, with the capital and entablature derived from Gibbs; figure (c) also has the simpler alternative form of Palladio which may commend itself particularly in small-scale interpretations of the order. Figure (d) shows the undiminished pilaster of the order, and demonstrates a central difficulty of pilaster design. Consistent throughout the plates is a column diminution of 0.075, and the face of the entablature aligned with the shaft of the column at its (projected) head. Since the pilaster is (unlike the column) normally undiminished, either the projection of the base mouldings must be increased, or the pilaster face must be proud of the entablature, otherwise the plinth of pilaster and corresponding column will not align. The base projection is unchanged in the example in figure (d), and the face of the pilaster is allowed to project beyond that of the entablature. If this solution is thought to be too noticeable, it is perhaps best to compromise by halving this projection and exaggerating the base mouldings by the same amount. Figure (d) also shows Palladio's entablature in section, indicating how the lower cyma sweeps into the soffit of the corona in an uninterrupted curve.

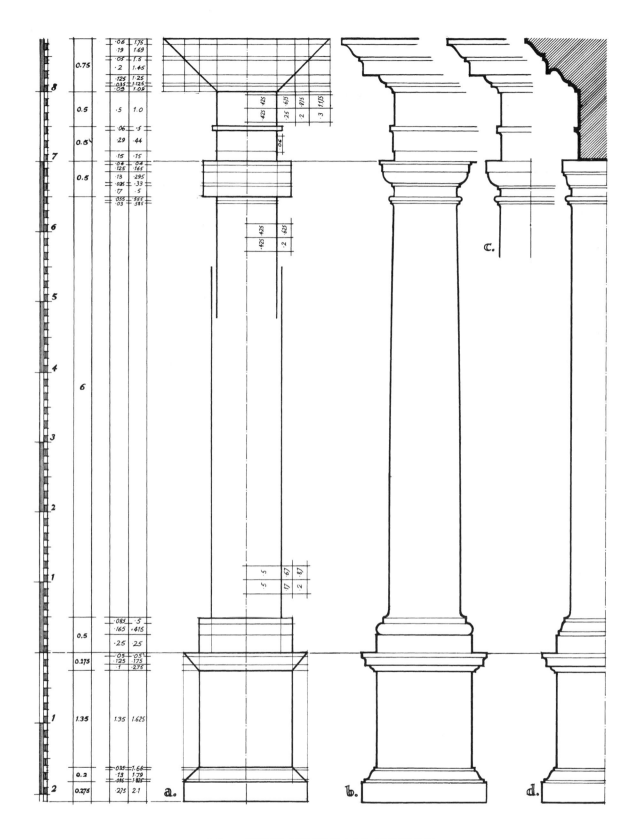

10.   THE TUSCAN ORDER

PLATE 11

THE TUSCAN CAPITAL AND ENTABLATURE

This plate shows the setting out of the Tuscan entablature in detail, and again shows both versions. A few specific points need to be noted. The capital is turned (circular on plan) up to and including the echinus. The abacus is never round on plan. In the Tuscan and Doric orders it is square, and in the Greek derived Ionic. In the other orders the shape of the abacus is derived from the square. The face of the entablature is aligned with the diameter of the notional upper limit of the column 'produced' through the capital, in accordance with Renaissance – but not earlier – practice. The projection of the cornice is equal to its height, so that the cornice profile is disposed about a line drawn at 45° from the upper end of the frieze. Most of the Renaissance authorities cited accept this height:projection ratio. Lutyens advocated a slightly steeper pitch, and there is a case in each specific application for this angle to be reassessed. It is well established that where oblique forms return through a right angle their pitch tends to be judged by the angle made by the mitre of the two adjoining faces – hipped roofs are a case in point – but as a general rule the angle of 45° will not lead one far astray.

As in plate 10, both Palladio's and Gibbs's form of capital and entablature are illustrated. The choice is for the individual – for applications which are restricted in scale, such as a porch, the simpler form of Palladio may be preferred, but in my view the more precise profile of Gibbs's corona with its undercut soffit is clearly superior. It is proper for the upper limit of the echinus in both Tuscan and Doric to be inset from the face of the abacus, but this inset should never be exaggerated, and in diminutive applications of these orders it can almost be dispensed with, in order that the abacus may not be seen to overhang the column too ponderously.

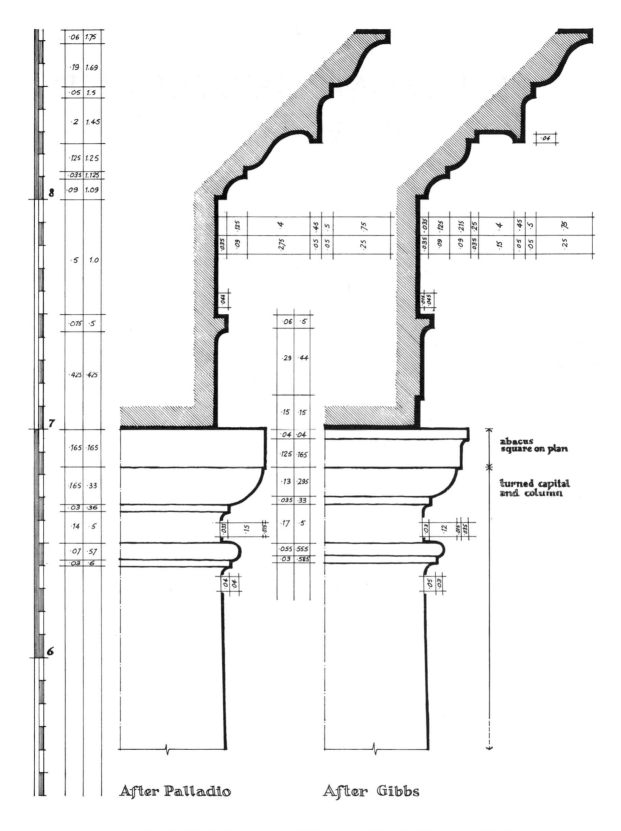

After Palladio   After Gibbs

11.   THE TUSCAN CAPITAL AND ENTABLATURE

PLATE 12

THE TUSCAN BASE AND PEDESTAL

Little comment is called for. As the plate indicates, I do not propose Serlio's arrangement with a circular plinth, which I think would look awkward and archaic to modern eyes. The column is circular in section down to and including the torus.

The mouldings of the pedestal are of the simplest form. The overall pedestal height, in accordance with the progression I have adopted for the orders as a series, is 2.1 diameters, or 0.3 of the column height. It is not normal for the Tuscan column to be fluted, or for either the die of the pedestal or the various mouldings to be ornamented in any way.

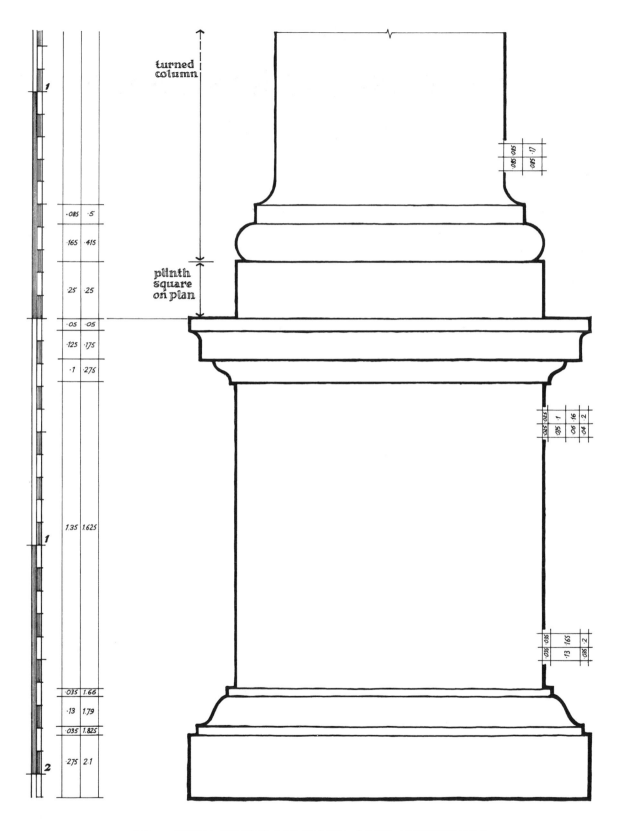

12.　THE TUSCAN BASE AND PEDESTAL

PLATE 13

THE DORIC ORDER

In setting out this plate I have deliberately chosen a spacing between the skeletal and the finished order of 3.75 diameters, so as to illustrate one feasible division of the frieze into triglyphs and metopes. I have followed Vignola, Gibbs (and Chambers) in allotting 8 diameters to the column and 2 to the entablature. The projection of the base, common to all my orders, is 0.67 diameters, but the capital, with its additional moulding surmounting the abacus, is allowed to project a little further (0.65) than the Tuscan capital from which it is clearly derived.

The proportions of the entablature – 0.5 for the architrave, 0.75 each for frieze and cornice – are accepted by most authorities. I have followed Gibbs and Vignola in leaving the architrave undivided; the intrusion into it of the regula and guttae corresponding with the triglyphs above provide sufficient decoration. Because of the arrangement of the mutules the cornice of this order necessarily has a projection greater than its height.

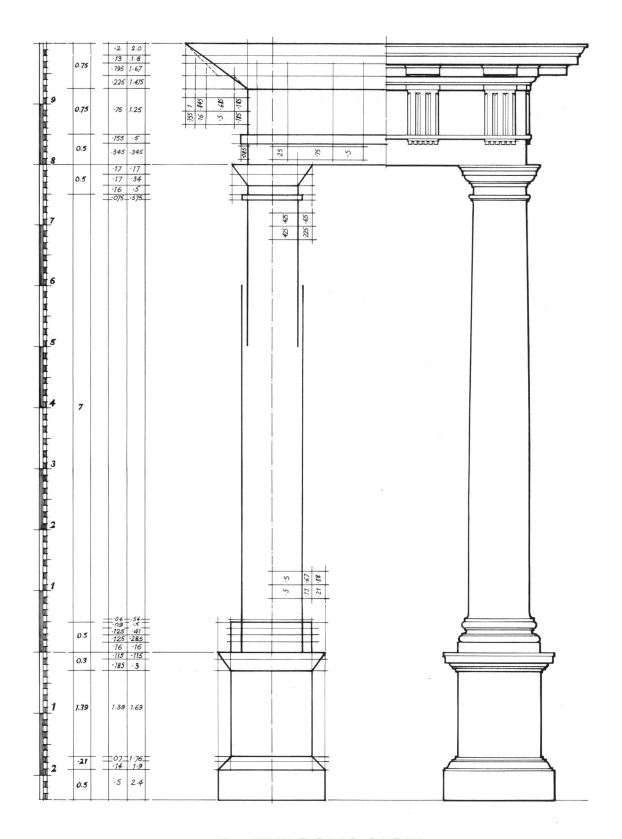

13.   THE DORIC ORDER

THE DORIC CAPITAL AND ENTABLATURE I AND II

Plate 14 shows the capital and entablature in elevation. The projection of the cornice is 1 diameter, compared with a height of 0.75, this being the only order in which the 'pitch' of the cornice departs from an angle of 45°. Indeed it is best to think of this cornice not as a 45° plane with mouldings cut into it, but as two separate series of mouldings separated by a broad soffit supported by the mutules. The mutules themselves are a series of hollow boxes in which a number of guttae or pegs hang down from a soffit, surrounding a solid block, as shown in plate 15, figure (a). Different authorities vary the size and number of the guttae, but the overall form seems to be generally agreed. Serlio shows a pleasing variation in his only example of the mutular form, where the hollow box is filled not with guttae, but with overlapping leaves carved in bas-relief. Chambers insists that the width of the mutule should correspond with that of the triglyph below, since 'the width of the rafter never exceeds the width of the beam of joist it stands on'.[18] I have followed Gibbs in the plate in making the mutule slightly broader, corresponding with the fillet above the triglyph. The forms are so far stylised that Chambers' assertion is a little pedantic. What is important is the design of the soffit. Plate 15 shows that it consists of square panels surrounded by a flat margin. The maintenance of a broad margin of consistent width is of more importance, and to narrow the mutule makes this more difficult. Plate 15(b) shows a section through the cornice with the sunk panel in its soffit. (Chambers, incidentally, substitutes a cavetto, for the crowning cyma, a pleasant alternative of slightly archaic appearance.) The soffit panels are often enriched with rosettes, darts, or geometrical patterns.

The frieze is quite awkward to set out. I have indicated how limited is the choice of suitable column spacings to allow a precisely square metope. Any departure from the precise square is likely to erode the characteristic appearance of the order.

The triglyph is one of the few elements not readily amenable to metric measurement, since it is divided into six parts, one part for each of the two channels, one for each of the three flat faces between them, and half a part to each chamfered edge. To accord with my decimal system I have allowed the overall breadth of each of the chamfered channels to exceed the intervening faces by a small amount. It will be seen from plate 14 that these channels terminate short of the top edge of the triglyph, leaving a plain upper margin. The upper limits of the channels are generally shown as square, though in Greek practice they were generally rounded in an elliptical curve. The metopes may be left plain or filled with bas-relief decoration, including *bucranian* masks, *paterae*, trophies or sculptured figures. Figure (b) in plate 15 explains in perspective the arrangement at the head of the triglyph.

18. Chambers, *op. cit.*, p. 50.

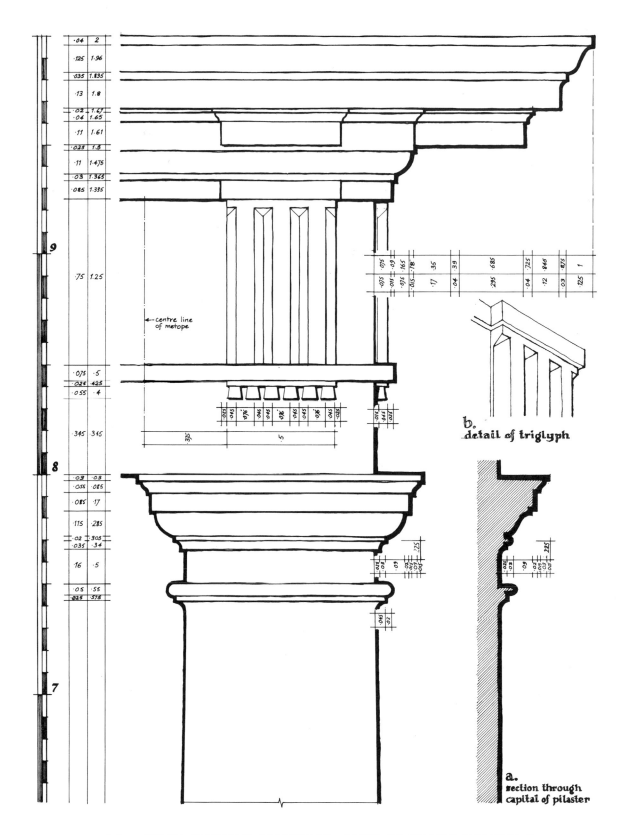

b. detail of triglyph

a. section through capital of pilaster

←--centre line of metope

14.   THE DORIC CAPITAL AND ENTABLATURE I

Beneath the taenia separating frieze from architrave, the regula projects, the same thickness and breadth as the triglyph with which it corresponds, exactly as if a tenon left on the lower end of the triglyph were passed through a mortice in the taenia. The regula, however, is plain, not reflecting the channelling of the triglyph. It is very shallow, and from it hang six guttae, conical in section, unlike those in the mutules which are cylindrical.

The capital, as shown in plate 14, considerably resembles that of the Tuscan order. However, beneath the echinus a cavetto is substituted for the plain fillet of the Tuscan, whilst the abacus is enriched by an additional *cyma reversa*. Figure (a) in plate 14 gives an appropriate profile for a responding pilaster, in which the echinus takes the form of a cyma. Plate 15, figure (c), gives an alternative form of the capital where the echinus rises from three oversailing fillets, and the neck of the capital is ornamented with rosettes and husks.

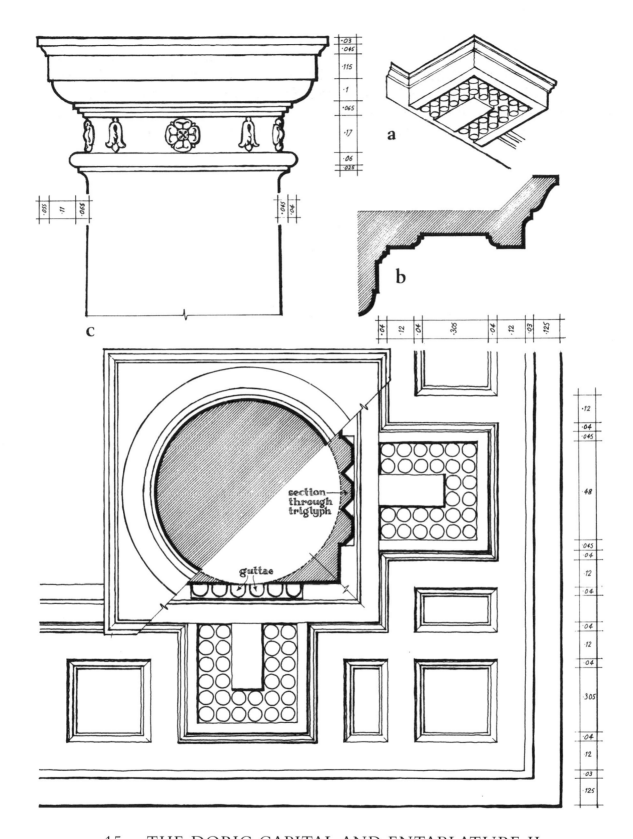

·03
·045
·115
·1
·065
·17
·06
·025

a

b

·055 ·11 ·055 · · ·045 ·04

c

·04 ·12 ·04 ·305 ·04 ·12 ·03 ·125

section through triglyph

guttae

·12
·04
·045

·48

·045
·04
·12
·04

·04
·12
·04

·305

·04
·12
·03
·125

15.   THE DORIC CAPITAL AND ENTABLATURE II

67

PLATE 16

THE DORIC BASE
AND PEDESTAL

As a proportion of 0.3 of the column height, the pedestal height totals 2.4 diameters. The corona of the capital is supported by a bold ovolo over a cavetto, and the base mouldings incorporate a scotia over the cyma reversa. The proportion of the die is again slightly over-square, very little different from that of the Tuscan order. The base shown is the classic *Attic base*, with two torus mouldings and an intervening scotia, separated by fillets. The fillet between base and shaft is excluded from the half diameter height allotted to the base.

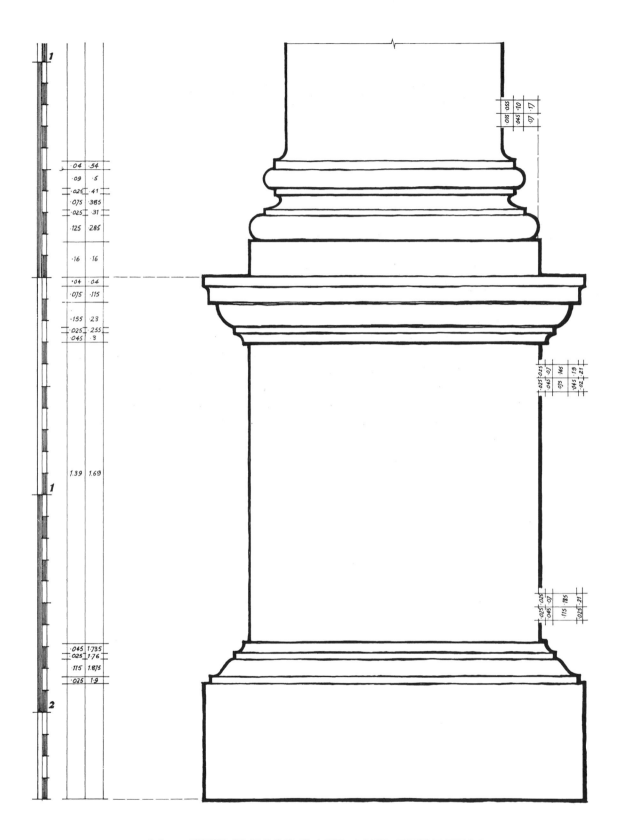

16.   THE DORIC BASE AND PEDESTAL

PLATE 17

THE IONIC ORDER

The order is again shown in skeleton form to give the principal dimensions, and full and half-columns are given at an intercolumniation of 3½ diameters between centres, together with the superimposed entablature. The column height of 9 diameters accords with most Renaissance authorities and with Vitruvius – half a diameter is allotted to the capital, and half to the base. One fifth of the column height produces an entablature height of 2.25 diameters of which, following Chambers, 0.675 is given to architrave and frieze and the remainder to the cornice. The projection of the cornice equals its height. The sequence of mouldings for the whole of the entablature is taken from Vignola, via Chambers, and I have ignored the modillion versions of Scamozzi, Palladio and others (Gibbs shows both modillion and dentil alternatives) in favour of the dentilled cornice which seems to me an admirable counterpart to the voluted capital.

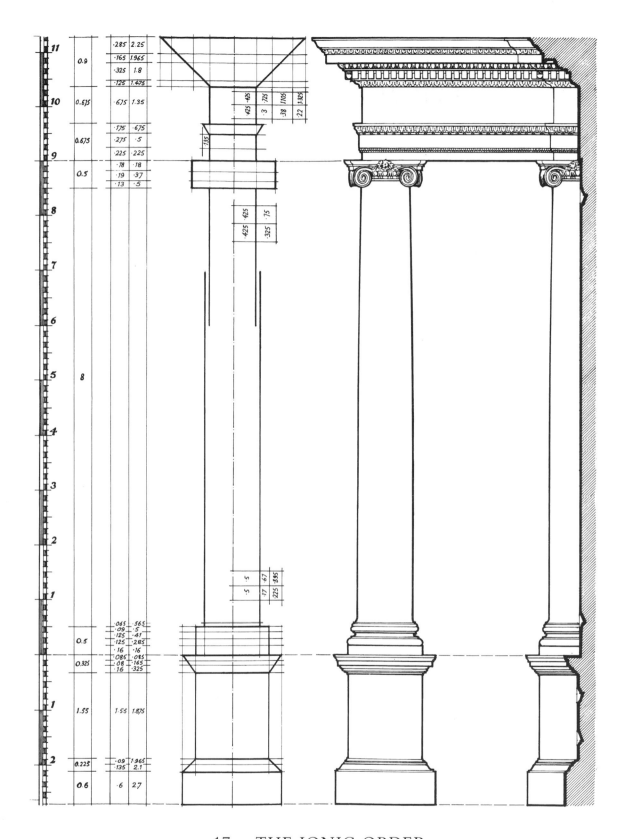

17.   THE IONIC ORDER

PLATE 18

THE IONIC VOLUTE

Most of the volutes I have drawn in the accompanying plates have been set out in the form described by Gibbs.[19] This is a comparatively easy method to set out, but produces somewhat abrupt changes of curvature at the junctions between adjacent arcs.

The method recommended by Chambers[20] gives a smoother curve and a more regular diminution of the width of the fillet. (Indeed, Chambers castigates Gibbs for the treatment of the fillet in his method, which involves short straight lines joining some of the component curves.)

However, Gibbs and Chambers agree that the breadth of the curved fillet should be one sixteenth of the total height of the volute.

To set out the volute proceed as follows:

1. Draw a vertical line FCB, F being the crown of the volute where it touches the abacus tangentially, C the centre and B the lowest limit of the eye. FC is 0.225 in length and CB 0.025.

2. With centre C and radius CB draw the circular eye (0.05 in diameter). Point A is the uppermost limit of the eye, where its circle intersects FC. Draw the horizontal diameter DCE.

3. Bisect the vertical radii CA, CB to give points 1 and 4.

4. With side 1,4 construct a square 1,2,3,4. Side 2,3 is bisected by point E. Draw oblique lines C2, C3.

5. Divide side 1,4 of the square into six equal parts, numbering the points thus established in the following sequence: 1, 5, 6, C, 12, 8, 4.

6. Draw horizontal lines through these numbered points to cut oblique lines C2, C3 at further numbered points 6, 10, 11 and 7. This arrangement is shown clearly in enlarged figure (a). A complete sequence of numbered points from 1 to 12 has now been established.

7. With centre 1, radius 1F draw the quadrant of a circle to intersect line 1,2 produced at G.

8. With centre 2, radius 2G draw the quadrant of a circle to intersect line 2,3 produced at H.

9. Continue in this manner drawing quadrants centred on the numbered points in sequence, each quadrant in turn determining the radius of the next, finishing with a quadrant centre 12, radius 12R, which merges with the eye at A.

The volute thus produced changes its radius at every 90° of rotation, giving a smooth enough curve for practical purposes.

19. Gibbs, *op. cit.*, plate 15.
20. Chambers, *op. cit.*, p. 53.

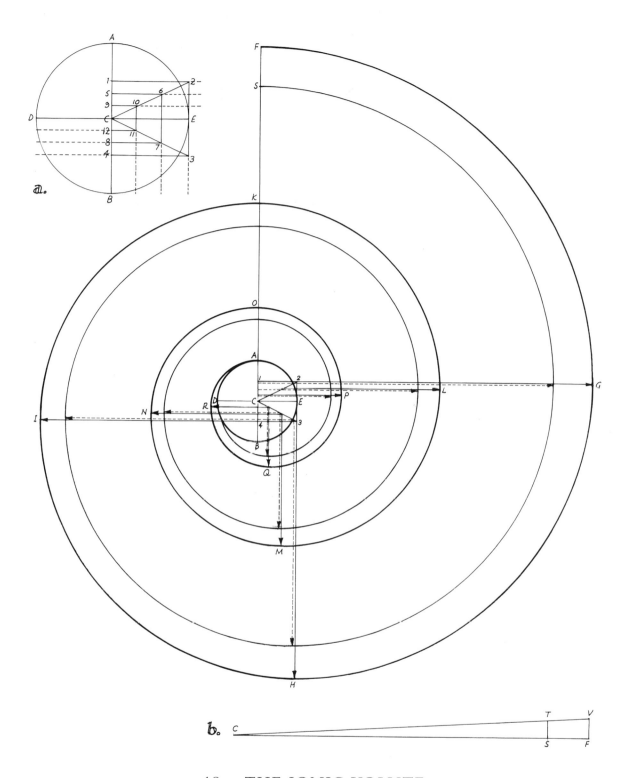

18.   THE IONIC VOLUTE

In order to produce the inner edge of the fillet similarly curved and steadily diminishing in width, the process is repeated using a second, slightly offset series of numbered points:

10.   As shown in figure (b), draw CF horizontally, measured from the main drawing, and draw VF vertically, equal in length to C 1. Join VC.

11.   Draw FS equal to the greatest desired width of the fillet. Draw a line vertically from S cutting VC at T.

12.   Take the length ST as equivalent to C1 to construct on line FB a slightly smaller square in the same manner as before, to establish the twelve numbered points for drawing the diminishing quadrants forming the fillet. The radii for this second series of quadrants are shown on the main drawing in broken line.

PLATE 19

THE IONIC CAPITAL AND ENTABLATURE

Plate 19 shows the setting out of the entablature in detail, and depicts the four-sided capital. Details of this and the alternative, directional capital are given in the succeeding plates.

It is difficult to decide whether the Ionic architrave should be of two faces or three. There is no consensus among the Renaissance authorities. Greek prototypes more often than not employ a triple division, but both Gibbs and Chambers reserve this more elaborate subdivision for the Corinthian, as the most decorative of the orders. I have followed this practice in the plate. It should be noted that the lower face of the architrave is considerably narrower than the upper – an equal division looks dull and is to be avoided.

The frieze may be either flat, as shown, or pulvinated, as in Palladio's Ionic in plate 6. The pulvinated frieze has a convex face, the centre of the curve lying on the column centre. If flat, the frieze may be enriched with bas-reliefs. All the principal mouldings are enriched with ornament – the extent to which this is applied depends on the scale and purpose of the particular design – except for the large crowning cyma and its terminal fillet, which are plain, certainly where an external order is proposed. The soffit of the corona is generally plain, though in external orders it may be weathered, with a drip moulding formed along its outer edge. At the corners, where the march of the dentils is necessarily interrupted, it is common for a circular ornament, often in the form of a pineapple or an acorn, to be suspended from the soffit.

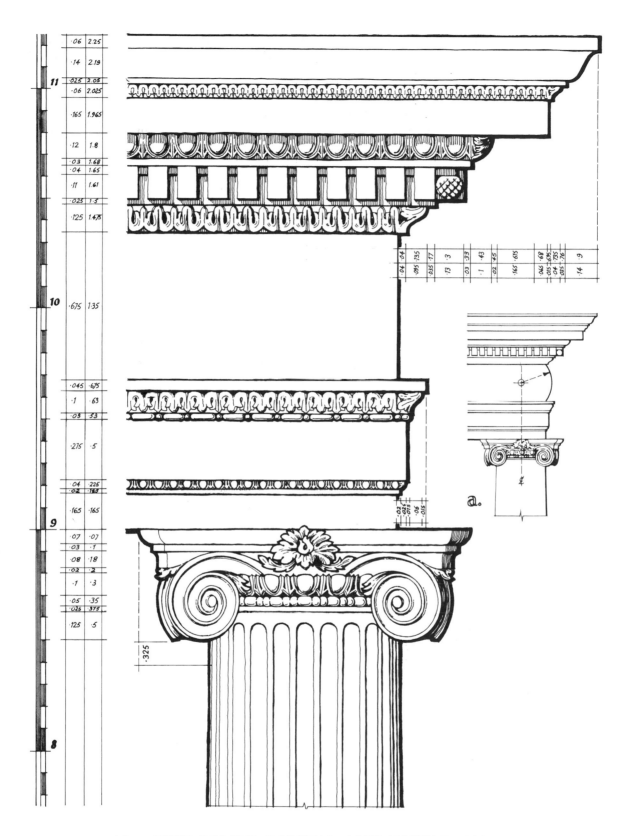

19.   THE IONIC CAPITAL AND ENTABLATURE

THE IONIC CAPITAL
I AND II

These two plates depict the two major alternative forms of the Ionic capital. Plate 20 shows the four-sided capital developed by Scamozzi, and plate 21 a parallel-sided capital from Greek and Roman sources. Ionic capitals are not difficult to set out once the drawing of the volute has been mastered, and there is a degree of latitude in the location of their essential elements.

Plate 20 shows elevations of the capital both from the side and across the diagonal. As the plan shows, the four double-sided volutes are arranged radially, the centre-lines of each pair being mutually at right angles, each at 45° to the plane of the face of the entablature above. The faces of the volutes close together at their extremities, and are inclined inwards slightly towards the bottom. The spiral fillet containing the volute moves gradually outwards from the face as it tightens so that the central eye stands proud of the rest. Each of the pairs is connected by a kind of web, and each pair stands clear of the ovolo and *astragal* mouldings which form a kind of extension of the column shaft and complete the essential construction of the capital. Ovolo and astragal are enriched with egg and dart and bead and reel respectively, the setting out related to a fluting pattern of twenty-four flutes to the shaft circumference, as shown on the plan. The abacus is moulded in three sections and has four main concave faces corresponding with the tapering volutes below and truncated by a short square face on the diagonal. The setting out of the abacus on plan corresponds with that for the Corinthian order, shown in plate 26. Each face of the abacus carries a central flower.

To draw the capital in elevation it is best to begin by marking out a series of horizontal lines to give the vertical subdivisions. Although the overall height of the capital is 0.5 diameters, this overlaps the shaft by a considerable amount, the upper edge of the ovolo being only 0.2 diameters below the top of the abacus. The eye of the volute should then be established. Vertically, it corresponds with the astragal around the head of the shaft. Horizontally it lies on the edge of the shaft profile, the centres of the eyes of each face of the capital being 0.82 diameters apart. The eye being established, the volute is then drawn according to the method preferred (plate 18, for example) noting that its upper sweep overlaps the lower element of the abacus right up to the lower edges of its central fillet, and then curves down to disappear behind the ovolo. Most authorities add, as well as the flower decorating the abacus, a small acanthus leaf under the abacus on the short diagonal face, and another trailing in the acute angle inside the upper sweep of the volute.

The Greek derived parallel-sided capital shown in plate 21 is different in a number of respects. The top of the shaft and its superimposed, concentric abacus and ovolo are similar,

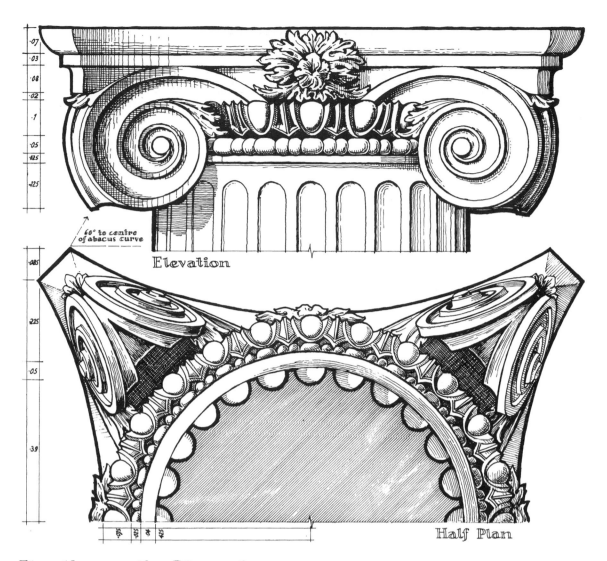

·07
·03
·08
·02
·1
·05
·025
·125

60° to centre
of abacus curve

Elevation

·085
·225
·05
·39

Half Plan

Elevation on the Diagonal

20.   THE IONIC CAPITAL I

though the ovolo itself is slightly less pronounced. The abacus is smaller than in the four-sided version, fractionally larger than the column diameter at 1.05 diameters overall, and is a plain square on plan, with a cyma reversa under a fillet. The volutes are similar in size, but on each principal face the eyes are 0.95 diameters between centres, giving an overall capital width of 1.35 diameters, as opposed to 1.5. The volutes are connected by a plain web which fills the space between abacus and ovolo, and each pair of volutes is joined across the end of the capital in a scroll of complex form, normally pinched upwards and inwards in the centre and hugging the rounded shape of the central astragal and ovolo. The abacus of either version may be enriched. Plate 21 shows a leaf pattern of Greek derivation. The parallel-sided capital is perhaps more appropriate to pilaster orders, where the omission of the back half of the capital is not obvious, but is awkward for orders which return on the flank of a building, unless the volute on the corner is pulled forward diagonally and given a second face, in imitation of a four-sided capital.

·03	·03
·07	·1
·115	·275
·085	·3
·05	·35
·025	·375
·125	·5

Elevation

·475 to centre of eye
℄ ·675 over volute

·525 over abacus

·055	·575
·07	·52
·075	·45
·29	·375
·085	·085

·056
·015

Half Plan

·425   ·045 ·035 ·08

End Elevation

21.   THE IONIC CAPITAL II

PLATE 22

THE IONIC BASE AND PEDESTAL

The Ionic pedestal has a height of 2.7 diameters (0.3 of the column height). The capital and plinth mouldings are quite complex: ovolo and cavetto separated by an astragal supporting a flat fascia with a crowning cynia reversa and fillet, and scotia and astragal over a cyma, to the plinth.

The die is somewhat elongated, having a height:breadth ratio of 1.16:1. The column base is again an Attic base, elaborated by an astragal added above the upper terns. Figure (a) shows the profile of the alternative Ionic base shown in the versions of Serlio, Vignola and Perrault in plate 6.

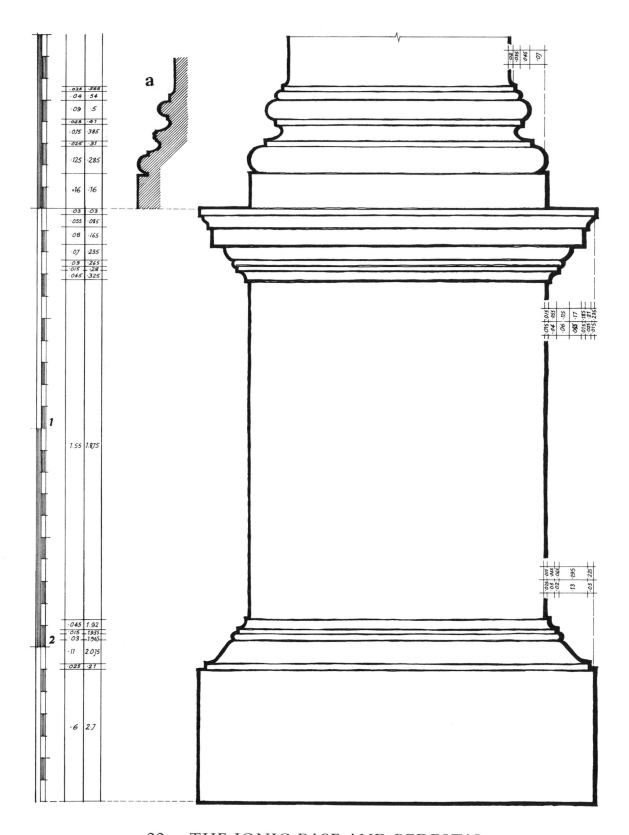

22. THE IONIC BASE AND PEDESTAL

PLATE 23

THE CORINTHIAN ORDER

The Corinthian again follows closely that of Vignola as interpreted by Chambers. The column, 10 diameters in height including the base and capital, and the entablature height of 2.5 diameters, or one quarter of the column height, avoids the cramping of the mouldings which constrains Gibbs's 2 diameter entablature. The skeleton drawing again shows the leading dimensions and indicates the overall envelope of the capital which takes the form of an inverted, truncated cone, bounded by the short diagonal faces of the abacus at the top, and the astragal terminating the plain shaft. The cornice has a projection equal to its height of 1 diameter, and architrave (in three steps) and frieze are allotted 0.75 diameters each.

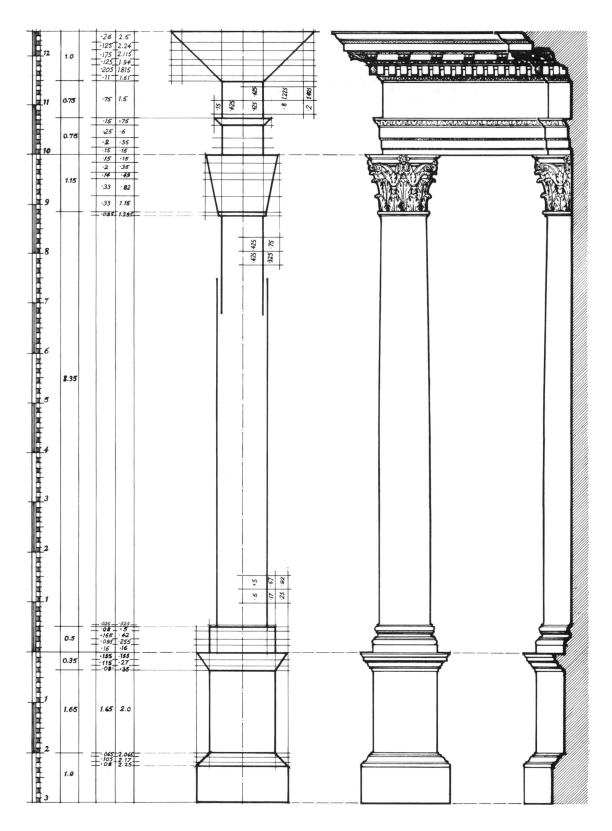

23.   THE CORINTHIAN ORDER

PLATE 24

THE CORINTHIAN CAPITAL AND ENTABLATURE

The Corinthian entablature may be regarded as the most elaborate and possibly the most elegant of all the orders. The frieze is flat, either plain or ornamented with bas-relief, and occupies 0.75 diameters. The same height is allotted to the architrave, in which the crowning cyma reversa, set over an astragal, tops a series of three diminishing planes, each separated by enriched mouldings. Whilst the projection of the cornice equals its height of 1 diameter, the projection and height of each of the component elements has to be precisely controlled if the sequence is to hold together correctly. A feature of the cornice is the pronounced overhang of the corona with its supporting consoles; in order to attain the right degree of overhang the mouldings below, a sequence of ovolo, dentils and cyma reversa, must be somewhat confined rather than following a more natural 45° pitch. The consoles are set at two-thirds diameter centres, another dimension not really amenable to decimal measurement, and it is desirable that a dentil should be centred below each. It will be observed that at a rhythm of three dentils to each console the dentils are about as widely spaced as can be allowed. The alternatives are either to allow four dentils to each bracket, which gives a rather crowded appearance, or to let the dentil course run independently of the console spacing, which may lead to difficulties in setting out. Mark Wilson Jones observes that the precise spacing of dentils and other repeated motifs is less important than the satisfactory resolution of the corners.[21]

Inset figure (a) shows alternative profiles for the upper part of the cornice, including the section of the sunk panel in the soffit. In the upper profile an additional drip has been introduced, suitable for an external order. To avoid disturbing the symmetry of the panel margin, the uppermost cyma and cyma reversa are somewhat compressed towards the vertical.

21. Wilson Jones, *op. cit.*, p. 29.

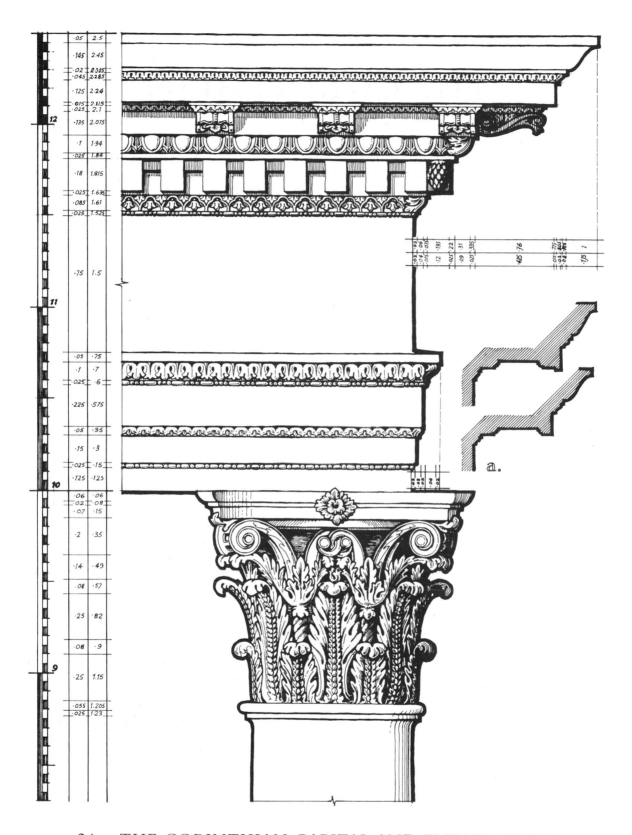

24.   THE CORINTHIAN CAPITAL AND ENTABLATURE

PLATE 25

THE CORINTHIAN ENTABLATURE

This plate amplifies the information set out in plate 24. The lower drawing shows the cornice in plan form. The configuration is dictated by the spacing of the consoles at two thirds of the column diameter. As in the Doric order, the exposed soffit between consoles contains a square sunk panel, with a flat margin of constant width. Unlike the Doric, however, where the mutules align over column centres, the spacing of the consoles is so contrived that there is also a square panel at the corner of the soffit. This satisfying arrangement depends on careful manipulation of the depth of the corona projection and the breadth of the consoles. Gibbs achieves it by some juggling of the console spacing whilst Chambers lets the consoles project right to the face of the corona, for a less attractive layout.

The upper figures show plan and elevations of a console. Because of the double volute and reverse curve this is an awkward pattern to set out. It is therefore most helpful simply to overlay my drawing of the side elevation with a square grid, each square measuring 0.01 diameters, amplified with the leading dimensions. The location of key parts of the elevation can be readily transcribed to any scale by drawing a similar grid and annotating the coordinates. The double volute is supported, and masked on its underside, by an acanthus leaf which grows from it and mirrors its general contours. Note that the flat face of the volute tapers slightly, being broader in the larger, base volute than in that at the extremity. On the end, the scroll is 'gathered' rather like the volute of the Ionic column.

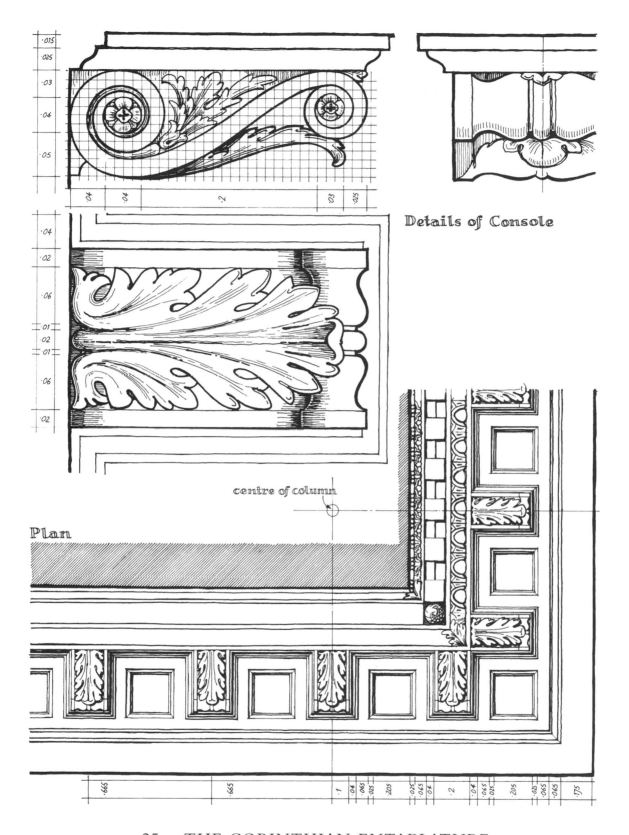

Details of Console

centre of column

Plan

25. THE CORINTHIAN ENTABLATURE

PLATE 26

THE CORINTHIAN CAPITAL

This and the Composite capital are the two most difficult elements to represent in the whole of the orders. The four sketches in the right-hand margin of the plate show the way the capital is built up. The core of the capital is a cylindrical continuation of the shaft, turned over at the top like the inverted mouth of a bell (glimpsed in the principal diagonal elevation) beneath an abacus of four convex sides in all respects similar to that of the four-sided Ionic capital. The abacus is supported by four pairs of volutes at the corners, and four subsidiary pairs in the centre of the sides, each pair joined by a web, often pierced and in turn supported by calyces or *caulicoli* springing from eight stems disposed around the column. The volutes in the centres of the sides are sometimes interlaced, as in the capital in plate 24. The capital is completed by two tiers of leaves – Chambers says that they should be of olive in the Corinthian order – again springing from the central cylinder, the whole of the lower part of which is thus concealed by foliage. A small flower adorns the centre of each side of the abacus. Unlike the volutes in the Ionic order, the sweep of the Corinthian volutes is contained beneath the abacus, the full depth of which appears on the elevation.

The vertical divisions of the capital are dimensioned in plate 24 and it is not necessary for these to be repeated in the more detailed plate. The total height of the capital, above the torus terminating the shaft, is 1.15 diameters, 0.15 being allocated to the abacus, the remainder disposed in three equal bands of one third of a diameter. The upper third is devoted to the volutes and calyces, and a band of leaves occupies each of the lower thirds. The extremities of the leaves are contained within a straight line drawn between the tip of the abacus and the torus surmounting the shaft.

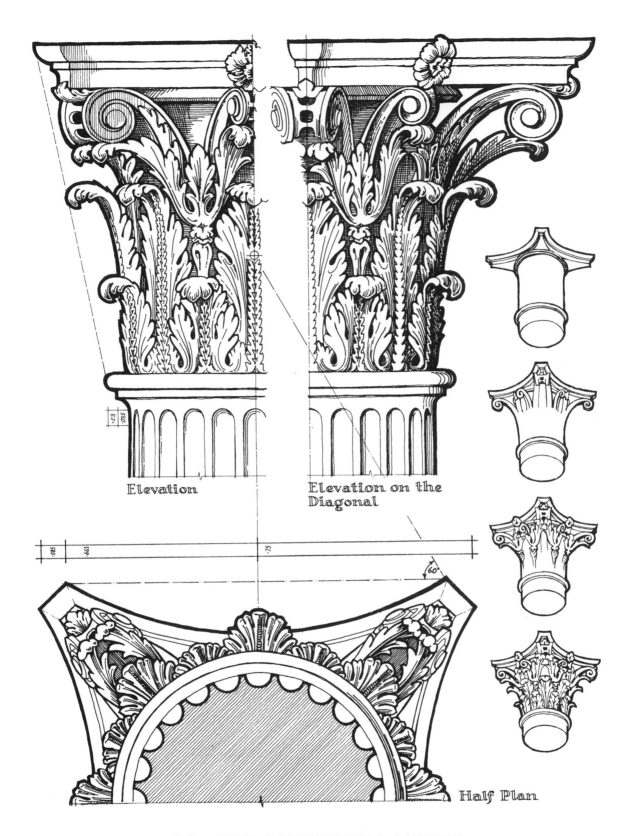

Elevation

Elevation on the Diagonal

Half Plan

26.   THE CORINTHIAN CAPITAL

89

PLATE 27

THE CORINTHIAN
BASE AND PEDESTAL

The pedestal, at 3 diameters, is 0.3 of the height of the column. The capital of the pedestal substitutes a cyma for the ovolo and astragal of the Ionic, and in the pedestal plinth the astragal is transposed from above to beneath the cyma reversa. The elongated die is often embellished, for example with a sunk panel on each face as shown in the plate, in this case with an enriched moulding, the section of which is shown on the right of the plate. The base of the column is an Attic base with astragals reinforcing the fillets containing the central scotia.

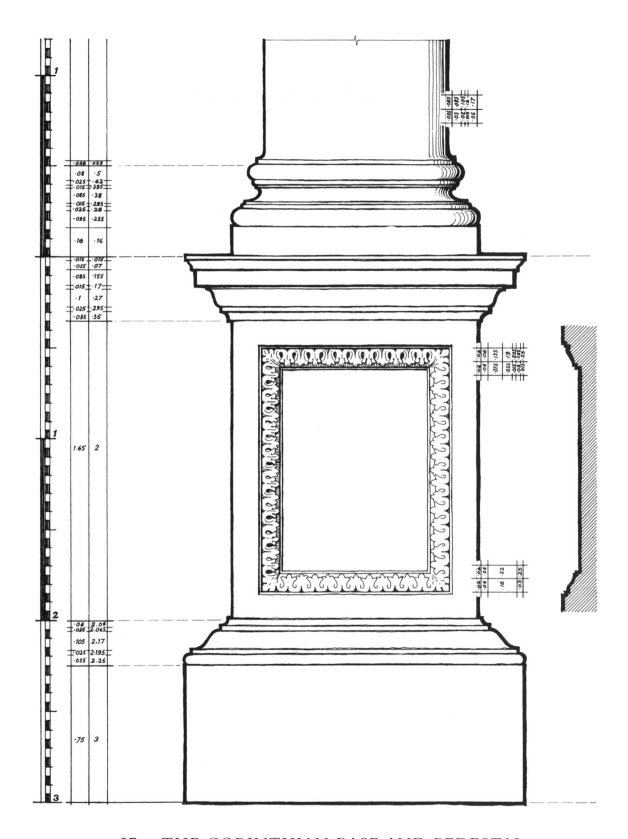

27.   THE CORINTHIAN BASE AND PEDESTAL

PLATE 28

THE COMPOSITE ORDER

The Composite order can be regarded equally as a variety of the Corinthian or a development of the Ionic. In overall proportions it follows the Corinthian exactly, having a column height of 10 diameters, with 0.5 allotted to the base and 1.15 to the capital; an entablature 2.5 diameters high with architrave and frieze each 0.75, surmounted by a cornice 1 diameter in height. As the plate shows, the capital, which is again contained in elevation within an inverted truncated cone, is less delicate than its Corinthian counterpart on account of its bold Ionic volutes. This somewhat coarser character is reinforced by the substitution of square modillions for the consoles in the cornice, as well as by the frequent employment of a pulvinated frieze.

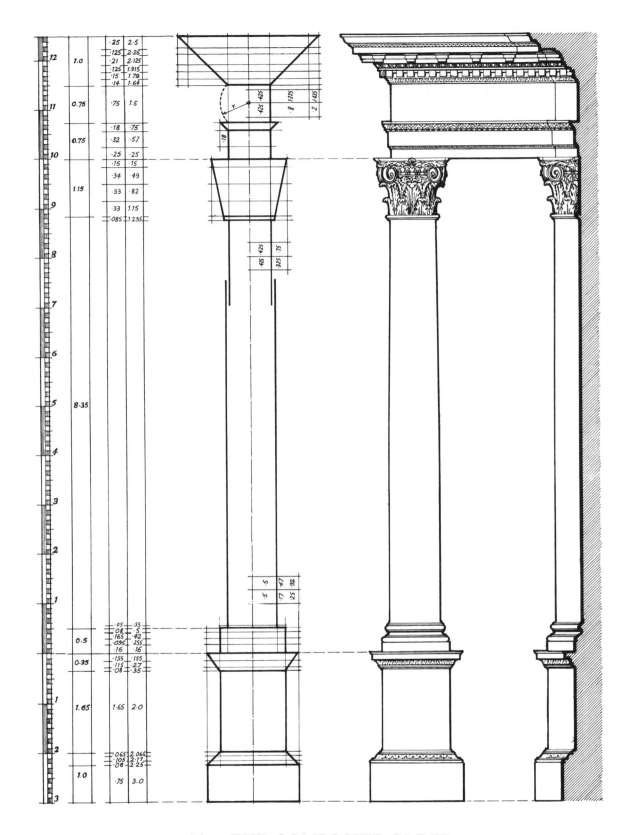

28.　THE COMPOSITE ORDER

93

PLATE 29

THE COMPOSITE CAPITAL AND ENTABLATURE

The capital, described in more detail in plate 31, consists in essence of a complete Ionic capital seated upon the lower two thirds of the Corinthian capital. In the interests of consistency, having finished the Ionic architrave with two unequal faces, I have divided the Composite architrave similarly, though the dimensions are here increased in accordance with the greater overall height of the whole entablature. The same constraints govern the projection of the lower members of the cornice as for the Corinthian: they are compressed in order to allow a generous width to the soffit of the corona. I have deliberately allowed some minor variations of dimensions between this cornice and that of the Corinthian if only to emphasise that these are by no means sacrosanct provided the dominance of such elements as the crowning cyma is not jeopardised. The profile adopted for this cyma and its supporting mouldings agrees with the upper profile in plate 24 (a), as for an external order, but as with the Corinthian order alternative sections are appropriate.

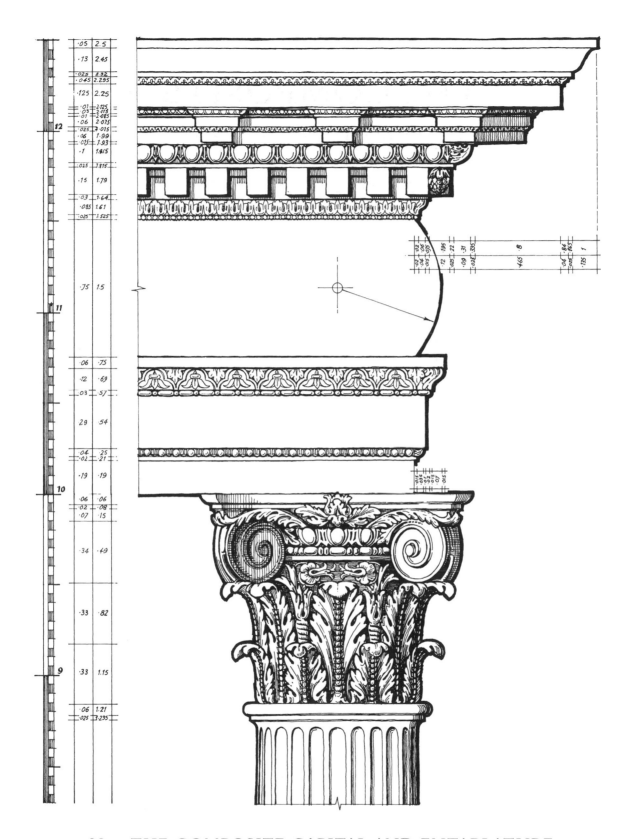

29.   THE COMPOSITE CAPITAL AND ENTABLATURE

PLATE 30

THE COMPOSITE ENTABLATURE

This plate amplifies the information contained in plate 29. Here again, the whole arrangement depends on the modillion spacing – two thirds of the column diameter – and the exact balance between modillion breadth and soffit width to produce an even margin around the panels of the soffit.

Figure (a) shows the arrangement of the dentil course at the corner, and is equally applicable to all the orders containing this feature. The two dentils at the corner leave a re-entrant which is filled with a rounded object – a pineapple, a fircone or an acorn is appropriate. The recesses between the dentils, it should be noted, are generally stepped, as indicated on the plan. The ovolo surmounting the dentil course generally turns the corner by means of a carved acanthus leaf, the decorated cyma and cyma reversa being similarly treated at the corner.

The upper section of the plate shows the arrangement of the modillion in detail. It consists of a stepped rectangular block of two faces separated by a cyma reversa. This and the crowning ovolo return along the intervening face between modillions in a similar manner to the cyma reversa surmounting the Corinthian consoles. The principal dimensions are indicated on the plate.

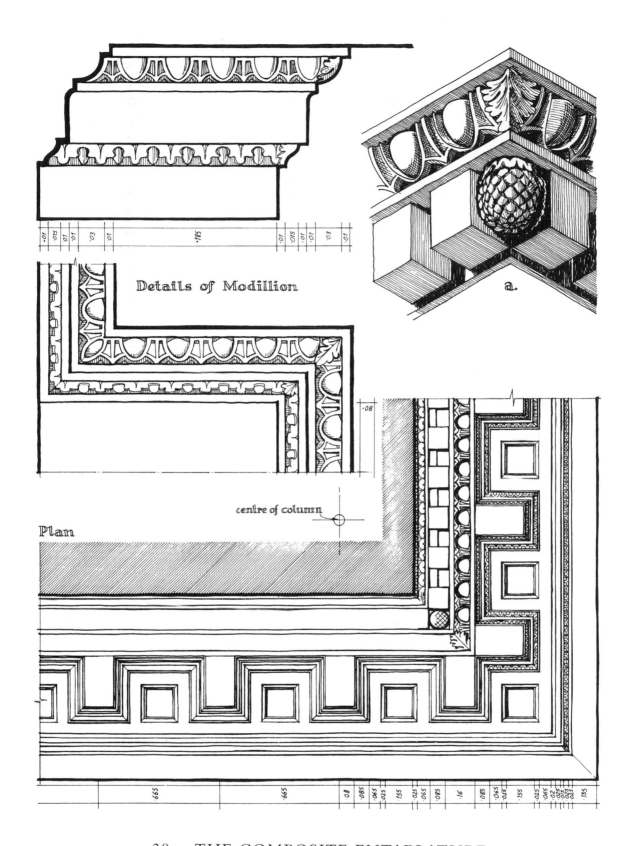

Details of Modillion

a.

Plan

centre of column

30.   THE COMPOSITE ENTABLATURE

PLATE 31

THE COMPOSITE CAPITAL

As has been said, this capital is a hybrid. The upper half consists of a complete Ionic capital – my dimensions (noted on plate 29) allow a slight variation in the height allotting it 0.49 diameters – over the lower two rings of leaves from the Corinthian capital. The only variation of the upper part from the true Ionic is a slight increase in the diameter of the concentric astragal and ovolo, to accommodate a belling out of the core of the extended shaft beneath. The version shown has rather more luxuriant foliage following the upper sweep of the volute which, as in the Ionic, obscures the lower face of the abacus. In the lower part of the capital, the stems of the calyces survive between the upper tier of leaves, but deprived of the actual calyces, sprout further small leaves and flowers on sinuous stems to decorate the belled portion of the core.

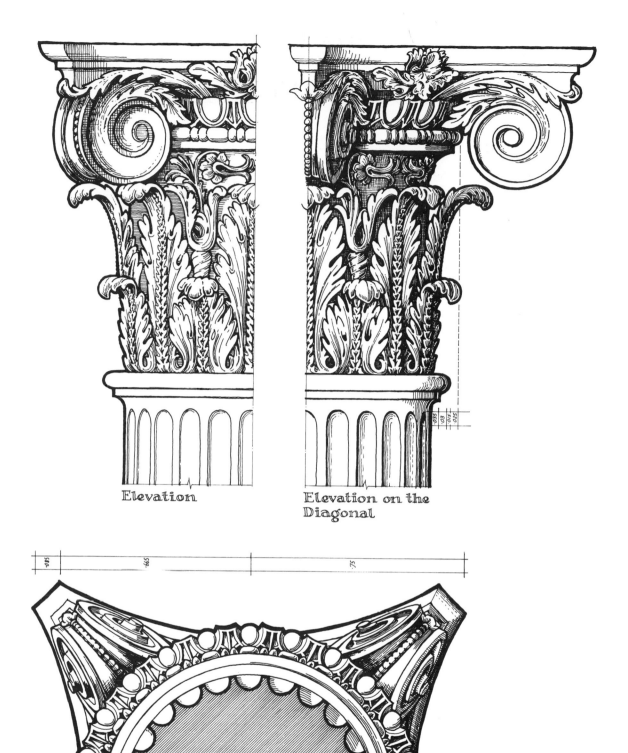

Elevation

Elevation on the Diagonal

Half Plan

31.   THE COMPOSITE CAPITAL

99

PLATE 32

THE COMPOSITE BASE AND PEDESTAL

The pedestal corresponds closely to that of the Corinthian order, and again is a hybrid development from the Ionic. The Corinthian proportions are followed exactly, but the pedestal plinth has astragals both above and below the cyma reversa, whilst the cornice has an additional astragal beneath the cyma. Similarly, the column base mirrors the Corinthian, but with an astragal between the upper torus and the fillet of the shaft.

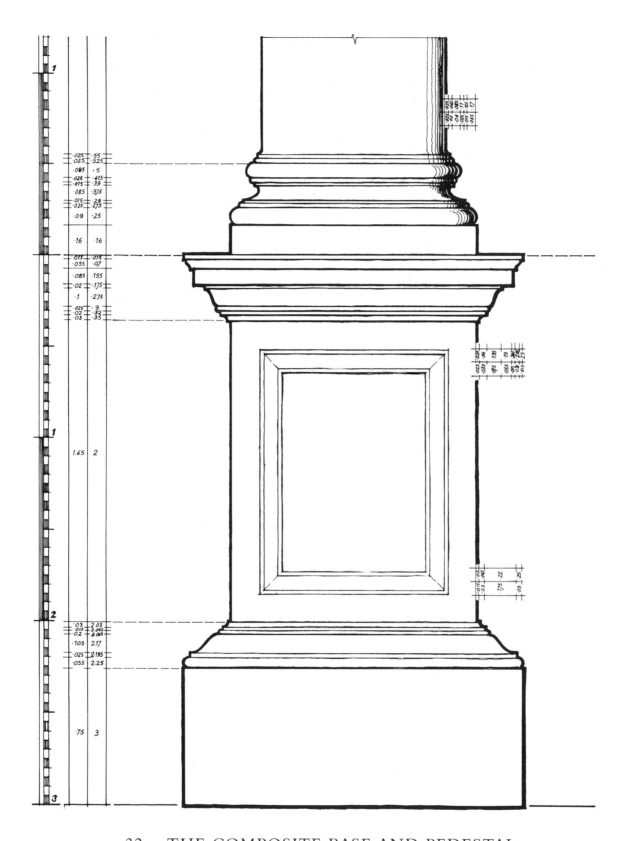

32.   THE COMPOSITE BASE AND PEDESTAL

PLATE 33

COMPARISON
OF
MOULDINGS

In the preceding plates describing the individual orders, I have endeavoured to show that there is a logical progression running through their sequence so far as the leading proportions are concerned. Within this progression, however, there is a considerable variety in the manner in which the minor elements are proportioned, and it is this variety which gives each order its individual character and prevents an undesirable uniformity from pervading the whole sequence. This is borne out by this plate, which represents an assembly of the comparable elements of each of the five orders.

Setting aside the capital, I have established four datum lines, one at the junction of architrave and frieze, one between frieze and cornice, the third at the foot of the column and the fourth on top of the plinth of the pedestal. The 'family likeness' of adjoining orders is immediately apparent. In terms of their entablatures, two groups may be distinguished. The Doric and Tuscan are very similar, sharing the same frieze height and simple corona profile, but the Doric is easily distinguished by its mutular form and the correspondingly greater overhang of its corona. Ionic, Corinthian and Composite share a more elaborate profile in the corona, and all have a dentil course. Again their multiple architraves with crowning cyma reversa are closely allied.

The Tuscan base is the odd man out, all the remainder being variations of the Attic base of two tori and a central scotia, with a sequence of additional astragal mouldings – though an Ionic base could be used as an alternative form in the 'major' orders. The mouldings of the pedestal form a similar steady progression. It is important that these should not be allowed too much delicacy – since the whole order rests on the pedestal it must display a degree of visual strength – so unlike the column bases, each successive pedestal is given a little additional space for its mouldings, so far as this can be afforded without jeopardising the stepped elongation of the die.

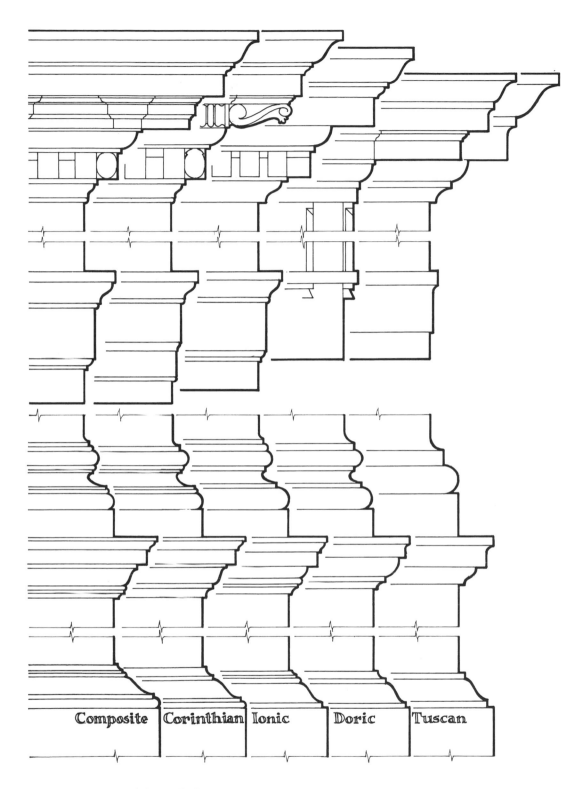

Composite Corinthian Ionic Doric Tuscan

33. COMPARISON OF MOULDINGS

103

JAMES GIBBS AND THE AMERICAN CLASSICAL TRADITION

Calder Loth

Senior Architectural Historian, Virginia Department of Historic Resources

34. James Gibbs, design for a round window, plate 110, *A Book of Architecture* (RIBA Library Photographs Collection)

If we were to name architects who had the greatest influence on the buildings of the English-speaking world, Palladio would undoubtedly head the list. Although it is tempting to put Sir Christopher Wren next, second place more realistically should be given to James Gibbs (1682–1754), a Roman Catholic Scot who was never part of the inner circle of the English architectural establishment of his day. Wren fashioned wonderful architecture, works treasured and praised since their completion, but he produced no books. To be a truly influential architect, it is necessary to publish. As much as the actual buildings, knowledge of architectural designs, theories, and ideas are spread through the medium of print. Palladio's villas and churches would certainly be admired to this day, but his influence over the past four centuries would have been minimal had he not produced his *Quattro Libri dell'Architettura* (1570). Gibbs produced books as well, only two, but both had an immense impact, particularly on the architecture of Britain's trans-Atlantic colonies, eventually to become the United States of America. In order to appreciate America's classical tradition, it is essential to understand Gibbs's role in it.

Gibbs was a highly gifted architect. His elegantly proportioned and carefully articulated buildings continue to please the eye as much as any erected in the British Isles. His mastery of his craft, however, was really made known to the larger world through his two publications: folios that crisply illustrated his own works, and also explained and demonstrated the proper use of the classical language of architecture. Gibbs's second work, *Rules for Drawing the Several Parts of Architecture* (1738), accomplished his ambition to provide a method for applying the classical orders that, as stated in his introduction, 'will be acknowledged by proper judges to be the most exact, as well as the easiest that has yet been published'. Indeed, not since Palladio's own exposition on the orders had instructions on the drawing and application of the classical language's vocabulary and grammar been presented so clearly and in a system so easy to apply.

Gibbs's method of determining the proportions of each element of the orders, as he justifiably claimed, was more simple and straightforward than any hitherto produced. It enabled architects and master builders throughout the country to execute classical details with ease. Moreover, Gibbs's interpretation of the five orders was happily one of the most beautiful ever presented. This is owing in no small part to the fact that Gibbs had spent a decade in Rome directly studying the ancient examples of classical architecture. There he was a pupil of the celebrated Roman architect Carlo Fontana, who was not only a leading practitioner of the more sober Roman Baroque style, but also an expert antiquarian. Gibbs was thus able to absorb the essence of Roman classicism, both ancient and modern, at its source.

Gibbs's *Rules of Drawing* became a standard reference on the classical orders for British architects and architectural students into the mid-twentieth century. As late as 1937, the Society of Architects in Britain sponsored the publication of a facsimile edition of *Rules of Drawing* for the benefit of practitioners, and reprinted it after the war. The impact of Gibbs's presentation of the orders and its long-term popularity is discernible in the special character of English Classicism – an assured patrician refinement not seen in most Continental works, which lean either towards the overly dramatic or towards a certain stolidity. Throughout Britain, as well as its former empire, hundreds of classical-style houses, churches, schools, and government buildings show the authority of Gibbs's *Rules for Drawing*, their architects having learned the principles and application of classical forms directly or indirectly from this eighteenth-century master. Indeed, the beauty and clarity of Gibbs's orders give them lasting appeal, and enable them to be a prime vehicle for expressing classical works into the future, as we will see.

Equally influential in its own way was Gibbs's earlier publication, *A Book of Architecture Containing Designs of Buildings and Ornaments*. First printed in 1728, this folio was an assemblage of building designs and details all by Gibbs; a catalogue of his own creations. It was a work of remarkable appeal: beautiful designs beautifully delineated. Few books of this ilk have had such lasting allure. Today, an original edition, if you are lucky enough to find one, fetches the price of a small automobile. Unlike Colen Campbell's *Vitruvius Britannicus* (1715–25), which was mainly a dossier boosting British architectural achievements, or the usual monographs of architectural firms, *A Book of Architecture*, was not meant to be solely an effort of self-promotion. It had a more high-minded purpose. In his introduction, Gibbs states unequivocally what he hoped the book would accomplish: '… that such a work as this would be of use to such Gentlemen as might be concerned with Building, especially in the remote parts of the Country, where little or no assistance for Designs can be procured.'

Gibbs thus wanted his illustrations to serve as models from which gentlemen or patrons, not having the benefit of skilled architects, could draw inspiration. They needed only to show to their local builders whichever Gibbs designs they preferred when planning their projects, be they country houses, churches, or even a monument. Whereas previous architectural publications had been concerned primarily with the theory and proportional systems of the classical orders, *A Book of Architecture* was one of the first 'pattern books' in the literal sense of the term, that is architectural patterns to be copied either in whole or in details, and in various combinations. Gibbs's designs are meant to speak for themselves. His descriptions of his plates are simply minimal identifications; for example: 'Plate XXIII. The West End' or 'Plate XXIV. The North Side, with plan in small.' Some go into more detail, describing the layout of floor plans and dimensions of rooms, but he offers no convoluted discussions of theory or proportion. In short, the designs are self-evident. They are meant to be visual demonstrations of what literate, properly ornamented classical design is all about, and provide patterns for those unable to procure custom schemes.

Gibbs illustrated in *A Book of Architecture* some of his most accomplished works alongside numerous unexecuted designs, as well as a variety of details: doorways, chimneypieces, monuments, and summer houses, even urns, cisterns, and stone tables for gardens. His building exteriors generally are exercises in restraint. Some of his smaller compositions, especially monuments and plaques, have a decidedly Baroque flavour, albeit with an English insouciance. Receiving primary coverage was Gibbs's most noted work, the church of St Martin's-in-the-Fields in the heart of London. Accompanying the engravings of St Martin's were plates showing variations on Wren-type 'wedding-cake' steeples. These steeple designs offer excellent illustrations of how a common vocabulary of motifs could be manipulated to make differing architectural statements. Furthermore, as Wren showed in his City churches, the variety of steeple designs had the practical effect of helping people distinguish one church from another in cityscapes crowded with churches.

A significant portion of *A Book of Architecture* was given over to country houses both grand and relatively plain – some executed, some conceptual. The more unpretentious houses owe much of their form and character to Palladio's villas. Palladian villas, however, were designed for a different climate and a different lifestyle. The hot Veneto summers dictated very high ceilings and relatively small window openings. Moreover, Veneto farming practices called for grain storage areas on the upper levels of many villas, resulting in very narrow openings just below the cornices. In a sense, Gibbs 'anglicised' the Palladian villa format by giving his country houses more horizontality through using larger window openings and lower ceilings, and providing upper-level bedrooms with requisite larger windows. The result was that Gibbs's country house designs became perfectly suited to Britain's eighteenth-century gentry lifestyle. The designs were clean, straightforward, and rational. In short, they became classics of house design and have shaped our notion of what a proper traditional house should look like ever since. Gibbs thus succeeded in making what he described in his introduction as 'Draughts of useful and convenient Buildings and proper

Ornaments' available to those who did not have the benefit of professional architects. As further stated, he indeed offered designs 'which may be executed by any Workman who understands Lines, either as here Design'd, or with some Alteration, which may easily be made by a person of Judgment'.

If Gibbs's intention was to serve gentlemen in the 'remote parts of the Country', we might ask what were the remote parts of the country in the first half of the eighteenth century. Gibbs likely had in mind the Scottish Highlands or England's West Country, regions far from large urban areas. Be that as it may, what truly were the remotest parts of the country in that period were the American colonies, a huge region of English civilisation on the far side of the planet. The colonies were as remote as any place could be, and truly were lacking in professional architects. Not until the British-trained Benjamin Henry Latrobe and George Hadfield began practising in the 1790s did Americans receive any but the most limited service from professional architects, as opposed to amateur 'gentleman' architects, or master builders. Indeed, barely a handful of true professional architects can be named as having worked in the American colonies.

British America was a unique phenomenon. Among other things, it was an effort to create a British civilisation in what was essentially virgin territory. To be sure, native Americans already inhabited the area, but unlike Mexico or Peru where the natives had highly structured societies with urban centres, the indigenous peoples of eastern North America were primarily hunter-gatherers. While they also practised a bit of primitive agriculture, they lacked what Englishmen then would regard as civilisation. To the English mind of the time, the native Americans were more of a nuisance, not a society with which to integrate. It was thus the settlers' task to establish a British-based culture and built environment on the vast land and its endless natural resources they claimed as their own. Despite causing the destruction of native-American culture, the English settlers did an impressive job of creating a 'new' England. Forests were cleared for farms and plantations, and well-ordered cities and towns were established on harbours and rivers up and down a coastline more than a thousand miles in length.

High-style architecture was a very low priority in the first decades of settlement. Though permanent English colonisation began in 1607, it was not until the beginning of the eighteenth century that the colonists began to move away from basic shelter and strictly vernacular forms, and become concerned about the image of their buildings. Even then, interest in achieving more refined architectural character in new construction was limited to the older established areas along the seaboard, well east of the frontier. In any case, hundreds and hundreds of new buildings were needed to accommodate the rapidly expanding population. America's first efforts at sophisticated public buildings and private residences were little more than provincial versions of Stuart and early Georgian works. Virginia's Governor's Palace of 1706 and Harvard University's Massachusetts Hall of 1720 were major accomplishments for their time and place, but they would hardly excite much interest had they been situated anywhere in England. Moreover, they reveal colonial America's need of trained architects and skilled artisans. Such early eighteenth-century works also tell of the want of good models, actual or published, for patrons and builders to study and copy. Seventeenth-century England produced few books on the art of building that offered any attractive ideas concerning the appearance of new structures. Those that were available were primarily treatises on the orders, or were concerned with the building trades, such as carpentry and masonry.

The West front of St. Martins Church.

Jacobe Gibbs Architecto. H. Hulsbergh Sculp.

35a James Gibbs, design for the west front of St Martin's in the Fields, plate 3, *A Book of Architecture* (RIBA Library Photographs Collection)

Enter Gibbs and his *A Book of Architecture* in 1728. This was not a 'how-to' work on how to construct a building. Instead, it showed in its seductive plates the latest fashions – what was 'in', and what a well-to-do individual could have by using the book in consultation with an experienced builder. It was merely necessary to pick though the pictures and select what appealed, and then work up a scheme with a master mason and/or master carpenter. The book was a godsend for a New World society, one collectively undertaking one of the largest building projects in history, amazingly almost completely without the benefit of professional architects. Both *A Book of Architecture* and *Rules for Drawing* found their way across the Atlantic. It is impossible to determine when the first copy of *A Book of Architecture* arrived on the American shores, but its influence, as well as that of *Rules for Drawing*, can be seen in colonial buildings constructed within a couple of decades of their publication.

The most conspicuous demonstration of Gibbs's influence on American architecture is found in churches. The demand for new churches in the colonies' growing cities and towns was obvious. Unlike the mother country, with its bountiful supply of medieval churches, the colonies had to start afresh. Gibbs's engravings of St Martin's-in-the-Fields, and to a lesser extent, Marylebone chapel, offered ideal models for houses of worship specifically tailored for Protestant worship. It would be no exaggeration to say that thousands of Protestant churches across the United States in some way owe their form or general appearance to Gibbs's prototypes. To Gibbs is due the credit for spreading the idea of a church requiring a temple-form body, fronted by a classical portico, and topped with a fancy steeple, the latter becoming the signature feature of church buildings in America. The interiors of St Martin's and Marylebone chapel were a complete break from medieval churches, with their divisions of nave, chancel and transepts. Gibbs's churches consisted instead of a simple rectangular space where one could see well, and especially hear well since the sermon became the highpoint of Protestant worship. The 'auditory' church thus became a favoured form for American Protestant churches big and small until the present day. Actual credit for developing the form should be given to Wren with his design for St James, Piccadilly and similar London churches, but Gibbs's publication did the job of popularising the type.

One of the earliest and most imposing American churches indebted to Gibbs's designs is Christ Church, Philadelphia, the principal house of worship of eighteenth-century America's largest city. The main body of the church was completed by 1739. The steeple, designed and built by the architect-builder Robert Smith, was added in the 1750s. Christ Church is a perfect illustration of how creative use could be made of Gibbs's illustrations. Forms and motifs are selected from various plates and assembled into an original composition. The interior is vaulted like St Martin's, but the supporting columns are Doric rather than Corinthian. The side walls are topped by an elaborate balustrade with urns following the engraved designs for St Martin's, but Christ Church's side elevations have two levels of orders rather than a single order projecting through both stories. The articulation of the two levels was probably picked up from illustrations in *Rules for Drawing*. In a complete departure from the standard pedimented ends of Gibbs's churches, Christ Church's east end is crowned with a Baroque motif based, of all things, on the attic of a garden seat shown on Plate 82 of *A Book of Architecture*. The niches in this design were applied to east end's lower level.

Christ Church was among the first of a series of important urban colonial churches indebted to *A Book of Architecture*. It was followed in Boston by King's Chapel (1749–54), by

35b James Gibbs, design for a garden seat, Plate 82, *A Book of Architecture* (RIBA Library Photographs Collection)

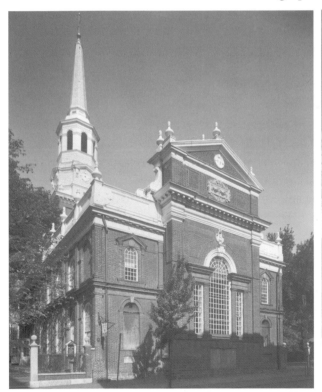

35d. St. Paul's Chapel, New York City (Historic American Buildings Survey)

35c. Christ Church, Philadelphia (Historic American Buildings Survey)

the able builder-architect, Peter Harrison, whose library included both *A Book of Architecture* and *Rules for Drawing*. The spirit of Gibbs is most evident on King's Chapel's interior, which has its galleries supported by paired Corinthian columns, rather than the single ones generally prescribed by Gibbs. New York City is graced by St Paul's Chapel, the oldest building on Manhattan Island. It was begun in 1763 by a Scottish architect-builder, Thomas McBean. The Ionic portico (on the east end) and the Gibbs-type steeple were added in 1794. With its lofty vaulted interior and in the handling of the classical details, St Paul's is perhaps the colonial church most faithful to Gibbs's style. Farther south, the 1750s St Michael's Church in Charleston, South Carolina, although somewhat heavily proportioned, also closely follows the St Martin's formula, having a steeple displaying the Ionic, Corinthian, and Composite orders in its several tiers, and a Doric portico sheltering the façade.

It would be safe to say that the majority of New England meetinghouses, directly or indirectly, owe much of their character to Gibbs. Dominating their towns and villages, these gleaming white wooden edifices have become icons of Americana, symbols of wholesome, small-town life. All have multi-tiered steeples, and many are fronted by porticos, freestanding, engaged, or implied. A classic example of the New England meetinghouse is the First Congregational Church of Litchfield, Connecticut, built in 1829, the third church on its site. Typical of Gibbs's church designs, and indeed of most of the American churches following his formula, the exterior is completely devoid of any religious symbols, a reflection of the Protestant anti-papist sentiments of the times. In the place of a saint or a cross, Gibbs's steeples, as well as the American versions of his designs, have a clock and a weathervane; municipal amenities to enable the townspeople to tell the time and the weather. Litchfield's church is no exception. Despite their wholly secular ornamentation, so strongly has the classical temple topped by a fancy steeple become associated with American church design, such buildings are immediately identifiable as works of religious architecture. The designer/builder of the Litchfield building is undocumented but it closely parallels churches in the Connecticut towns of Milford and Avon by the master builder, David Hoadley.

Perhaps the meetinghouse most closely following the St Martin's format is Asher Benjamin's festive and highly sophisticated First Congregational Church of 1814, on Connecticut's New Haven Green. With its red-brick walls and bright white trim, First Congregational is a wonderfully American evocation of St Martin's, steeple and all. It even does St Martin's one better by having the pedestals of its surrounding balustrade crowned with urns. Similar urns were planned for St Martin's balustrade, but were never installed. Although he consistently employed Roman orders and details on First Congregational Church, Benjamin moved with the trends, and ultimately became America's leading populariser of the Grecian style.

Gibbs's influence on colonial American domestic design can be seen throughout the former thirteen colonies. Many houses exhibit window and door treatments, as well as other details, that can be traced to both of his books. Several noteworthy examples, however, have façades and layouts based directly on Gibbs's schemes. The most striking parallel is the plantation house at Mount Airy, in Richmond County, Virginia. Built in the 1750s for the planter John Tayloe, the rusticated centre pavilion with its arcaded loggia is copied directly from Gibbs's design for a house for 'a gentleman in Dorsetshire', illustrated on Plate 58 in *A Book of Architecture*. The floor plan and curved wings connecting the dependencies

36a   First Congregational Church, Litchfield, Connecticut
(Historic American Buildings Survey)

36b First Congregational Church, New Haven, Connecticut
(Historic American Buildings Survey)

37a.   James Gibbs, design for a gentleman in Dorsetshire, plate 58, *A Book of Architecture* (RIBA Library Photographs Collection)

37b.   Mount Airy, Richmond County, Virginia
(Historic American Buildings Survey)

likewise closely parallel the plan on Plate 55, for a country house in Essex. Though John Tayloe was among the wealthiest men in the colonies, Mount Airy's dwelling house is relatively small by English standards. Mount Airy, however, was not a small operation. Such a plantation would have had several dozen support buildings spread over the estate. Only the master and his family occupied the main house. The service areas such as kitchen, laundry, office, schoolhouse, and servants' (slave) quarters were located either in separate buildings or attached dependencies. Had all these functions been gathered under one main roof, the result would compete in size with one of the behemoths in *Vitruvius Britannicus*. But such architectural grandeur was costly, impractical, and inconsistent with colonial lifestyles, particularly in the southern colonies. The more compact house designs of Gibbs, rather than the palaces of William Kent or Colen Campbell, proved more adaptable to the American situation.

Mount Airy's designer remains undetermined. Circumstantial evidence points to one John Ariss (also spelled Oriss and Orliss). About all that is known of Ariss is that he at one time lived not far from Mount Airy, and that in 1751 he ran an advertisement in the *Maryland Gazette* stating: 'By the Subscriber (lately from Great Britain) Buildings of all Sorts and Dimensions are undertaken and performed in the neatest Manner, (and at cheaper rates) either of the Ancient or Modern Order of Gibbs' Architect.' Ariss cannot be documented as having worked at Mount Airy, but the advertisement at least proves a local individual was using Gibbs's books for his compositions.

Two other plantation houses in eastern Virginia; Blandfield and Mannsfield (the latter destroyed by Civil War shelling in 1863), are directly inspired by schemes in *A Book of Architecture*. Both houses were built in the 1770s, and were based on Plate 63, a house design for 'a Gentleman in Yorkshire'. In 1796, the architect Benjamin Henry Latrobe visited Mannsfield and described it as being in the style of the country gentlemen's house in England of fifty years ago. Latrobe was accurate in his assessment. Mannsfield and its Virginia companions could fit comfortably in the English countryside as modest mid-eighteenth-century manor houses. Even though the designers of these Virginia plantation houses remain anonymous, the main lesson of these structures is that they would not appear as they do had not Gibbs's books been available at the time. The author of *A Book of Architecture* thus succeeded in his goal to provide a useful work for people in remote areas where practising architects were not available.

The individual responsible for fitting up some of the *interior* of Mount Airy, however, is known. William Buckland, born in Oxford in 1734, and trained as a carver-joiner, arrived in Virginia in 1755 as an indentured craftsman. His first commission involved the completion of the interiors of Gunston Hall, the home of George Mason, author of the Virginia Declaration of Rights. In 1762, Buckland was recorded as being paid for work at Mount Airy. Although the house was gutted by fire in 1844, surviving fragments of original woodwork parallel the bold detailing of Buckland's work at Gunston Hall.

In 1771, Buckland moved to Annapolis, the capital of Maryland, where he displayed his design skills in at least two of the town's grand mansions. His masterpiece, for which he should be credited as architect, is the Hammond-Harwood house. For much of the detailing of this elegant work, Buckland made ready use of *A Book of Architecture*, one of the numerous architectural works listed in his inventory. The Rococo surround of the pediment window is clearly inspired by the designs on Plate 110 (see p. 105). The arched

38a.   Hammond-Harwood House, Annapolis, Maryland
(Historic American Buildings Survey)

38b.   James Gibbs, designs for niches, plate 109, *A Book of Architecture*
(RIBA Library Photographs Collection)

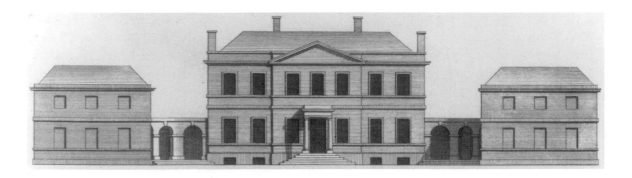

38c.   James Gibbs, design for a gentleman in Yorkshire, plate 63, *A Book of Architecture*
(RIBA Library Photographs Collection)

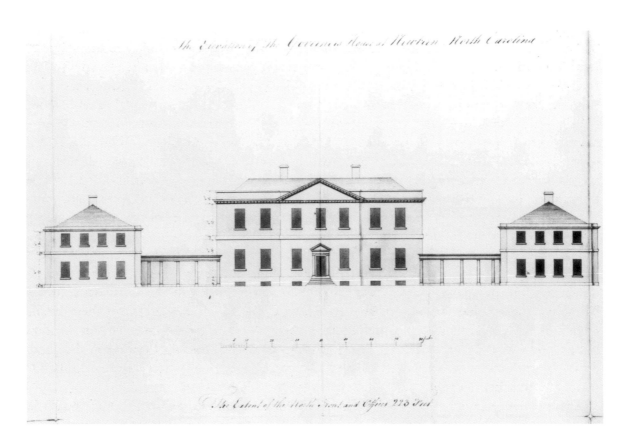

38d.   John Hawks, design for Tryon Palace, New Bern, North Carolina
(Courtesy of Tryon Palace Historic Sites and Gardens, North Carolina
Department of Cultural Resources)

stairway window with its rusticated frame was probably based on the windows shown in Gibbs's elevation of the east end of St Martin's in the Fields. The list of motifs could continue, but these examples sufficiently demonstrate the use this talented artisan made of James Gibbs's illustrations. Interestingly, the Hammond-Harwood house aedicule doorway, surely one of the most beautiful of the period in either Britain or America, closely parallels a doorway design in Abram Swan's *The British Architect* (1758), also a book owned by Buckland. This design, however, combines elements from several of Gibbs's designs for niches found on Plate 109 of *A Book of Architecture*. Like many eighteenth-century pattern books, *The British Architect* borrows freely from Gibbs's work.

Colonial America's grandest and most ambitious work of domestic architecture, one almost totally reliant on a Gibbs country house design, alas does not survive. This was the official residence of William Tryon, the royal governor of North Carolina, erected in the port town of New Bern. Tryon arrived in New Bern in 1764, determined to have himself properly housed in a residence that would also be the colony's seat of government. He brought with him the architect John Hawks, a Lincolnshire native who had trained under Stiff Leadbetter, who later served as Surveyor of St Paul's Cathedral. In 1767, Hawks prepared the drawings for a building to accommodate the governor's public and private quarters along with the council meeting room and accompanying offices. The elevation of the final design of the North Carolina Governor's Palace, also known as 'Tryon Palace', was copied almost precisely from Plate 63 of *A Book of Architecture*, the same plate that inspired the design of Blandfield. As with Plate 63, the palace's central two-storey block was connected to two-storey dependencies by low, curved hyphens. The plans of both the central block and the dependencies, however, were deeper than the Gibbs design, in order to accommodate the additional requirements of an official residence. Following Independence, the capital was moved from New Bern to Raleigh. Tryon Palace stood neglected, and eventually burned in 1798. A faithful reproduction of the palace on its original site, using Hawks's elevation and plan, was constructed in the 1950s.

The several houses noted above would not be conspicuously different from other academic Georgian dwellings had they been situated in England. More distinctly colonial, however, were the scores of clapboarded timber-frame houses of the northern colonies. These products of local housewrights also have a Gibbs presence in many of their details. As with the New England meeting houses, their wooden construction, green window blinds, and sun-dappled siding give them an unmistakably American character, the products of a land where wood was in endless supply. Gibbs-style classical touches, applied to regional vernacular forms, produced a charming local idiom.

An illustrative example of colonial American vernacular with Gibbs's flair is the 1760 Elisha Sheldon house, also in Litchfield, Connecticut. Here, the pedimented centre bay is composed of an engaged Ionic colonnade, above which is a Palladian, or Venetian, window. This combination of elements can be found in a façade design on Plate 43 of *A Book of Architecture*, described by Gibbs as 'A Draught of a House made for a Gentleman in 1720'. The combination of a Palladian window above an engaged colonnade in a pedimented central pavilion can be found in several American colonial works. Whether the builder of the Elisha Sheldon house was inspired by Gibbs firsthand or secondhand cannot be nailed down, but it can be said that Gibbs is the ultimate source for the house's appearance.

39a.   Elisha Sheldon House, Litchfield, Connecticut
(Historic American Buildings Survey)

39b.   James Gibbs, draught made for a house for a Gentleman in 1720, plate 43, *A Book
of Architecture* (RIBA Library Photographs Collection)

Other examples of this Palladian motif centre-bay treatment are found in the Deming house, also in Litchfield, and in the Cowles house in Farmington, Connecticut. These houses ultimately became icons of colonial design, and inspired the façade treatment of numerous Colonial Revival houses erected in the first half of the twentieth century.

A common feature found on both the exteriors and the interiors of many of America's more high-style colonial buildings, is the Ionic order using a capital with angled volutes. This type of capital has ancient precedents, most notably the Temple of Saturn (known in the eighteenth-century as the Temple of Concord) in the Roman Forum. But ancient capitals with all four volutes set on the diagonal are rare. Most ancient Ionic capitals use parallel volutes, as seen in scores of reused ancient capitals in numerous early Christian churches. Palladio considered parallel volutes to be the purer Roman form, and illustrated only that type in his *Quattro Libri*. When Palladianism became the fashion for the Whig aristocracy in eighteenth-century Britain, the capital with parallel volutes was decreed to be the proper Ionic form. A leading proponent of Anglo-Palladianism, Sir William Chambers, illustrated the parallel volute Ionic as the correct Palladian type in his *Treatise on the Decorative Parts of Civil Architecture* (1759). Chambers admittedly included an illustration of the angular Ionic, but it is shown mainly as an aside.

It was Palladio's contemporary, Vincenzo Scamozzi, who developed a partiality to angular Ionic, using it in many of his own works and promoting the form by publishing it in his own architectural treatise: *L'Idea dell'Architettura Universale* (1615). Scamozzi eventually became a preferred authority on the orders for Continental architects; hence the Ionic with angled volutes became the dominant version of the Ionic, particularly for French Renaissance works. While the British aficionados of Palladio stuck to their parallel volutes, Gibbs apparently admired the more Baroque quality of the angled volute capital and presented it as the only model for the Ionic in *Rules for Drawing*. The form was illustrated in detail in plates XIV and XV, with instructions on how to draw it provided on pages 12–14. As Gibbs increasingly became the authority on how to execute the orders, Chambers notwithstanding, the angular Ionic became the preferred Ionic for most early and mid-Georgian buildings.

The primacy of the angular Ionic in the eighteenth century does not mean that all master builders and craftsmen were referring directly to Gibbs's book when using the order. Gibbs was a victim of his own success. During the eighteenth century the restrictions against plagiarism were notably lax, if they existed at all. Gibbs's version of the orders, along with his other published details, attracted numerous contemporary pattern book writers including Batty Langley, William Halfpenny, Abraham Swan, and William Pain. As noted above, many of Swan's details are derived from Gibbs. But it was Batty Langley, more than any other, who shamelessly plagiarised designs for his various pattern books, many directly from Gibbs, including the architectural orders, as well as window and door treatments. He even went so far as to sign his plates, including that for the angular Ionic, 'Batty Langley Invent. 1739'.

Scholars of Georgian architecture in both Britain and America, particularly the latter, are constantly faced with the problem of determining whether an architect or builder was obtaining his knowledge of the orders and other details directly from one of Gibbs's books or from a work by authors such as Langley, who helped themselves to Gibbs's efforts. While

40a.   John Edwards House, Charleston South Carolina
(Historic American Buildings Survey)

40b.   James Gibbs, 'The Ionick Capital,' plate XIV, *Rules for Drawing*
(RIBA Library Photographs Collection)

plagiarism is considered a bad word, Gibbs's plagiarisers in fact had the effect of disseminating one of the most successful and attractive versions of English classicism. Even though they may have been derived second- or third-hand, be that as it may, the orders, as well as many details found on scores of Georgian buildings, both in Britain and America, ultimately owe their appearance to James Gibbs.

The Ionic order, specifically the angular Ionic, is a case in point. In colonial America, the Ionic became the order of choice for upscale works. Doric was considered somewhat stern for domestic buildings. Corinthian, with its elaborate leafy capitals, proved to be beyond the ability of most colonial artisans to execute; hence it is rarely seen except in the most ambitious works. The interior columns of New York's St Paul's Chapel or King's Chapel, Boston are conspicuous examples of the rarely used Corinthian. The Ionic, however, was ideal for houses and other buildings where the master builder or patron wanted a touch of sophistication. Doorways, porch columns, and pilasters inside and out, from New England to Georgia, employ the Gibbs-style angular Ionic. Notable examples are the dwarf portico sheltering the entrance of the 1768 Jeremiah Lee Mansion in Marblehead, Massachusetts, the pilasters in the splendid 1753 stair hall of Carter's Grove near Williamsburg, Virginia, or the columns supporting the porch of Charleston's John Edwards house.

As with other Gibbs architectural forms and motifs, the angular volute Ionic was picked up by pattern-book writers other than Langley, and published almost verbatim, thus further spreading its use. It even appeared in some of the earliest American-produced pattern books, such as those by Asher Benjamin and Owen Biddle, as the proper form of Roman Ionic. Indeed, it became so specifically associated with early America's traditional architecture that in the early twentieth century, when the colonial revival movement came into full swing, the angular Ionic was the espoused form of Ionic. Molded composition capitals of this type were manufactured and sold through builders' supply companies throughout the country. Front porches and doorways in cities and towns everywhere in the United States were embellished with Gibbs's Ionic, though it is safe to assume that 99% of both the manufacturers and customers of such capitals had no idea of who ultimately was responsible for introducing the form to America. Whatever, tens of thousands of twentieth-century Gibbs-style Ionic capitals adorn the nation's buildings. Such capitals remain readily available through architectural supply and ornament companies today, continuing Gibbs's influence nearly three centuries after their introduction.

Although Gibbs, through his devotees, influenced the image of American classicism for much of the eighteenth and early nineteenth centuries, the colonies, and later the states of the new nation, were not entirely devoid of more strictly Palladian proponents. Chief among these relatively few was the famous statesman and remarkable self-taught architect, Thomas Jefferson. So entranced was Jefferson by Palladio, particularly his exposition on the orders, that he proclaimed the *Quattro Libri* to be 'the Bible'. In Jefferson's masterpiece, the University of Virginia complex, the Ionic capitals he employed in the professors' pavilions, save for one discreet example where the angular Ionic is used, are derived from Palladio and were ordered from Italy, where they were carved in Carrara marble. Jefferson also preferred the use of Palladio's Ionic in his first, major work, the Virginia State Capitol, in Richmond, but he gave in to Charles-Louis Clerisseau, his mentor on the project, who advocated the angular Ionic. Because the Capitol's portico is two bays deep, the use of the

41a.   James Gibbs, design for a temple in the Doric order, plate 67, *A Book of Architecture* (RIBA Library Photographs Collection)

41b.   Monticello, Albemarle County, Virginia (Robert C. Lautman, Courtesy of The Thomas Jefferson Foundation)

angular volute type allowed, the capitals of the portico's side columns to be consistent with the front ones. Indeed, Clerisseau referred to them as Scamozzi capitals; obviously no mention of Gibbs from the Frenchman.

Jefferson's veneration of Palladio did not mean that he disdained other approaches to classicism. His library held more titles on architecture than any other private library in America, and included both *A Book of Architecture* and *Rules for Drawing*. In his rebuilding the west front of his home, Monticello, with its dome and portico, some scholars have led us to believe that Jefferson was inspired primarily by the Hotel de Salm in Paris, a building he greatly admired and which has a hazy similarity to Monticello. Though Jefferson makes no mention of it, the west front of Monticello has a more than coincidental resemblance to Plate 67, a design for a garden temple in *A Book of Architecture*. Both feature an octagonal dome with stepped plinth set on a drum punctuated with round windows. Both also have a tetrastyle Doric portico with a full Doric entablature continuing around the whole building. Jefferson was really little different from other builders and architecturally literate clients of his day, in that he picked and chose what he liked from various sources and combined them in novel ways for his own schemes.

In one instance, however, it is possible to illustrate an undeniable borrowing by Jefferson from a Gibbs design. Jefferson intended to embellish the grounds of Monticello with pavilions and follies displaying various architectural styles, even Gothic. Regrettably, he never got around to building them. Among the drawings in his own hand for these ornamental structures is one for a pavilion consisting of free-standing columns supporting a stepped pyramidal roof topped by an urn. Jefferson lifted the stepped roof and urn directly from a pavilion design on Plate 77 of *A Book of Architecture*.

Jefferson's Monticello represents one of the most famous and familiar houses in America. No less famous or recognisable, however, is the White House, the official residence of United States presidents. The White House was mainly the inspiration of George Washington. He felt it necessary for the home of the new nation's chief executive to be of sufficient size and dignity to inspire respect for the office. It was Washington himself who selected the winner of the design competition, a scheme by the Irish-born architect James Hoban. Even in this famed icon of American architecture, the Gibbs influence dominates. Hoban is said to have modelled his White House design after Leinster House, the 1740s Dublin mansion designed by Richard Cassels, now the seat of the Irish Parliament. Leinster House would have been well known to Hoban; it and the White House do share a likeness.

An equally strong similarity exists, however, between the White House, as originally built, and Plate 53 in *A Book of Architecture*, a design for an eleven-bay country house at Seacomb Park in Hertfordshire. Like the White House, the Seacomb Park design has an engaged pedimented portico employing the angular Ionic order. (The present projecting White House porticoes were added in 1824 and 1829.) Leinster House, on the other hand, employs the Corinthian order, but it shares with the White House the alternating triangular and segmental pediments above the windows of the principal floor. The alternating pediments are a relatively common treatment on Renaissance-style buildings, beginning in England with Inigo Jones's Banqueting House. Gibbs made frequent use of them on his façades, perhaps most famously on the Cambridge Senate House.

42a.   James Gibbs, design for a house at Seacomb Park, plate 53, *A Book of Architecture*
(RIBA Library Photographs Collection)

42b.   James Hoban, N. elevation, The White House, Washington, D.C.
(Maryland Historical Society)

A Gibbs touch is also evident in Hoban's drawing of the White House north elevation, where the basement windows have rusticated frames, a treatment which is referred to in Britain as a 'Gibbs surround'. These Gibbs surrounds were executed, and survive on the White House today. Like the alternating pediments, the rusticated frame was not a Gibbs invention, but he popularised it through his frequent use of it for his own works such as St Martin's-in-the-Fields, and through illustrations in his two books. Gibbs surrounds are found in America not only on the White House but on a number of high-style colonial-era buildings, mainly churches, including St Paul's Chapel.

All of this is to say that while we cannot document a direct connection between Gibbs and the White House via Hoban, Gibbs presents in his book the image of a restrained but dignified classical mansion with remarkable similarities to both the White House and Leinster House. Hoban obviously drew inspiration from Leinster house, but it is impossible to think that he did not have access to *A Book of Architecture* as well. The book was certainly available in Charleston where Hoban designed the South Carolina Statehouse before moving to Washington. Moreover, his statehouse design has more than a coincidental resemblance to a design for a house façade on Plate 54 of *A Book of Architecture*. Both this Gibbs design and the statehouse design have nine-bay elevations, conspicuously punctuated by round and oblong niches inside the end bays. Both elevations also have an engaged tetrastyle portico above a rusticated basement. In summary, as with many American works, one can say that neither the White House nor the South Carolina Statehouse would have acquired the appearance they did without Gibbs's book.

The impact of the White House on America's architectural psyche has been significant. Its quiet stateliness established a standard for many of the nation's imposing mansions. While some individuals have dared to erect copies, the White House has remained more an ideal, a symbol both of democratically elected authority and elegant domesticity. It is a grand house but not an ostentatious palace. It impresses but does not intimidate, and offers appropriate accommodation for America's chief executive. This world-famous architectural symbol, whose image is readily available in people's pockets on the nation's currency, owes a great debt to Gibbs. Gibbs did not design royal or ducal palaces, but rather commodious seats for gentlemen. As he himself wrote, the aesthetic effect of his houses came through 'the Proportion of the Parts to one another and to the Whole, whether entirely plain, or enriched with a few Ornaments properly disposed'. Hoban's White House design is consistent with Gibbs's stated intent: 'that these Designs should be done in the best Tast[e] I could form'.

With the entry of Classical Revivalism and the romantic styles onto the American architectural scene in the early 1800s, the Gibbs influence began to wane. Even the White House was old-fashioned for its time. Exceptions were the New England meetinghouses, which continued to follow the St Martin's format well into the nineteenth century, particularly with their fanciful tiered steeples. It was not until the turn of the twentieth century that America witnessed a resurgence of interest in Renaissance forms, primarily French and Italian, and to a lesser degree those of eighteenth-century England. The Beaux-Arts influence dominated the scene, mainly because America's leading architects were trained at the École des Beaux Arts in Paris, and also because most American architecture schools adopted the Beaux Arts method for architectural education. Beaux Arts classicism was based chiefly on Giacomo Vignola's *Regola delli Cinque Ordini d'Architettura* [*Canon of the Five Orders of Architecture*] (1572 edition). Most American-trained architects learned their orders from Vignola's treatise or later versions of it. Gibbs remained largely an outsider in this period.

In 1902, William R. Ware of Columbia University produced a textbook on the orders entitled *The America Vignola*. In his preface, Ware proudly proclaimed: 'Other systems have been presented by Alberti, Palladio, Scamozzi, Serlio, Sir William Chambers, and others. But Vignola's Orders have generally been accepted as the standard.' Ware's book, with his orders based on Vignola's proportions and detailing, subsequently became the primary means by which the classical architectural language was taught in American schools. Vignola's classicism varies from Gibbs's in that it has a certain stolid quality, resulting from greater emphasis on entasis in the column shafts rather than diminution. Gibbs, on the other hand, has Palladio and Scamozzi as his standards, and refines their interpretations of the orders to produce what connoisseurs of the art might regard as a more visually satisfying version. The differences are subtle to be sure, but they are the types of subtleties oenologists note in fine wines, subtleties that make a difference and greatly affect character, especially for those with sophisticated tastes.

Ware, however, admitted some recognition of Gibbs's contribution with his *Rules for Drawing* when he stated in his preface: 'After the chief part of this volume was in press my attention was directed to a somewhat similar work by the celebrated James Gibbs.' 'He published in London in 1732, a series of plates showing the Orders and their applications with a brief descriptive text.' Ware quoted from the introduction to *Rules for Drawing* Gibbs's intention to produce a method for drawing the orders that would be most exact and easiest. But Ware closes his preface to *The American Vignola* with the gratuitous statement: 'I find on examining the [Gibbs] plates that, though they follow an entirely different system, they have anticipated some of the methods in the present work'. It may be worth mentioning that in the inventory of Gibbs's fine arts library of over 150 volumes, Vignola's treatise is not listed.

While the Beaux Arts style, along with Vignola's orders, dominated America's architectural scene in the early twentieth century, a Gibbs look began to appear here and there in various up-market works, particularly in some of the mansions erected by American plutocrats. The driving force behind this English image was the Anglophilia that increasingly permeated American high society. Staggering new fortunes generated a desire for the traditional trappings of wealth and position: great houses, elaborate gardens, and works of art. The English-style country house presented the ideal backdrop for these instant gentry, and Gibbs's houses were quintessentially English. To be sure, other evocations of Old England, most notably the Tudor mode, found their way to American's exclusive suburbs and countryside, but it was the dignity and elegance of eighteenth-century English architecture, so handsomely handled in Gibbs's works, that was especially engaging. The American establishment identified with the mother country. America's heritage was largely rooted in England, and Americans viewed the grand mansions of the Augustan Age as the American colonial house carried to its logical conclusion. An architect who well understood this was Horace Trumbauer (1868–1938). Like most proficient architects of his day, Trumbauer could produce accomplished works in any number of styles: Gothic, Tudor, French Renaissance, or American Colonial. However, in the rural reaches of his native Philadelphia, Trumbauer designed several country houses that illustrated a keen understanding of the Gibbs mode.

43a.   James Gibbs, design for a house to be built in Greenwich, plate 47, *A Book of Architecture* (RIBA Library Photographs Collection)

43b.   Whitemarsh Hall (destroyed), Wyndmoor, Pennsylvania
(Pennsylvania State Archives)

Trumbauer's Whitemarsh Hall, completed in 1920 for Edward T. Stotesbury, near Wyndmoor, Pennsylvania, would have made Gibbs proud. More than other mansions of its ilk, Whitemarsh Hall effectively demonstrated how designs in *A Book of Architecture* could be adapted for gentlemen in 'the remote parts of the country'. This splendid structure closely paralleled Plate 47, an unrealised design by Gibbs for a country house in Greenwich. In applying monumental classicism to a residence, the danger always exists of having the structure appear as a public building. Trumbauer, like Gibbs, was able to employ a restraint and warmth that made Whitemarsh Hall immediately recognisable as a grand residence and not a post office. The domestic elegance was aided perhaps by adding urns to the balustrade and inserting a pediment window with a Baroque foliated frame, both standard Gibbs touches. The portico departs slightly from pure Gibbs by its use of Palladian-type parallel volutes in its Ionic capitals rather than angular volutes. Sadly, like so many of estates of its era Whitemarsh Hall succumbed to suburban sprawl, and was ultimately demolished in 1980.

Sir Edwin Lutyens also referenced to some degree the same Plate 47 in his design for the garden front of the British Embassy in Washington, DC, completed in 1928. Lutyens gave his building a decidedly Anglo-American look by the use of red brick for the wall surfaces and black-green louvred blinds framing the windows. He also did not fail to employ the angular Ionic order. A Gibbs influence can certainly be seen in many of Lutyens' British works, particularly his banks, but it would not be a stretch to assume that Lutyens was aware of the strong influence of Gibbs on American architecture when he determined the basic character of his embassy design.

At the same time that architects such as Trumbauer were looking directly at European and English models for inspiration, the United States was witnessing a widespread interest in the architecture of its own past, primarily that of the colonial era. The Colonial Revival movement brought on many versions of American eighteenth-century buildings, many so freely interpreted that their source of inspiration is sometimes difficult to identify. As the Colonial Revival movement matured, architects became more faithful in their interpretation of authentic models. Such noted colonial houses as Mount Vernon and Westover, or the Tory mansions of Cambridge, Massachusetts, saw versions of themselves appearing in the enclaves of the well-to-do throughout the country. More informed architects, however, were able to put themselves in an eighteenth-century mindset by going back to the sources for colonial design, such as the books of Gibbs, Robert Morris, Abraham Swan, and Batty Langley, and using their illustrations as a basis for their own adaptations of the colonial idiom. These exercises produced some surprisingly sophisticated compositions, works on a par with much of the neo-eighteenth-century architecture being erected in Britain in the same period.

A leading proponent of this Anglo-colonial style, and one who well understood the potential for creativity through informed historicism, was the New York architect, William Lawrence Bottomley (1883–1951). Bottomley's earlier works were adapted directly from English models. A particular favourite of his was Mompesson House in Salisbury Cathedral Close. The warm formality and comfortable scale of this early Georgian house made it ideal for translation into modern American residential works. But as Bottomley's practice matured, he became ever more conscious of the importance of respecting America's architectural heritage, and acknowledging it as a design resource of great potential. Bottomley

44.   Milburne, Richmond, Virginia (Calder Loth)

was quick to realise that some of the best American colonial architecture owed a debt to Gibbs. Gibbs-inspired houses such as Mount Airy and Blandfield became design resources for several of Bottomley's most successful domestic works.

Milburne, one of Bottomley's several suburban villas along the James River in Richmond, Virginia, is an excellent demonstration of a synthesis of colonial Virginia plantation architecture and designs by Gibbs. Begun 1934, Milburne owes its general outline and façade design to Plate 63 in *A Book of Architecture* (see p. 118), the same plate on which Blandfield and Tryon Palace were based. Bottomley, however, sprinkled Milburn's exterior with details from other plantation houses: the doorway from Wilton, the garden arcades from Mount Airy, and brickwork typical of fine colonial Virginia houses such as Carter's Grove. Equipped with all the modern conveniences, houses such as Milburne have become classics of American domestic architecture, and remain today as popular and visually appealing as they were the day they were completed.

The list of American architects of the early and mid-twentieth century who displayed an understanding of Gibbs and wove his forms and details into their designs is a long one. A short list would include not only Trumbauer and Bottomley, but Delano and Aldrich, Philip Trammell Schutze, Charles A. Platt, John Russell Pope, Mott. B. Schmidt, and Walker and Gillette, all of whom gave America wonderfully literate works with Gibbs touches. Such architects were long shunned by historians but are at last enjoying overdue recognition. The stultifying impact of Modernism on the American architectural scene for decades inhibited rightful appreciation for such quality and beauty; a beauty that comes from an understanding and mastery of a perfected architectural vocabulary.

The teaching of the classical language of architecture all but ceased in America, as well as everywhere else in the Western World following World War II. This was the result of the takeover of architectural education by instructors with a Modernist agenda. The causes of this stylistic revolution have been endlessly discussed and will not be dwelt upon here. But it needs to be pointed out that despite academe's continuing disdain for classical architecture, the overwhelming majority of individual houses being built in America today are in traditional styles, many of them employing a classical vocabulary. Regrettably, virtually all of the works in this latest generation of traditional-style residences employ the classical architectural vocabulary with little understanding of the rules. The designers of these inept attempts at sophistication, whether they are builders or architects, have had no training in the classical language. Details are picked out of books, magazines, and catalogues, and applied with no recognition of proportional systems or the rationale of the classical orders' various components. Yet these neo-traditional designs continue to be in high demand and dominate the housing market. However embarrassing they may be, such 'homes' honestly strive to give a sense of time and place to a society that is quickly losing its sense of time and place. This architectural illiteracy principally afflicts domestic design, but many traditional-style churches, commercial buildings, and civic works are similarly deficient in the refinement once taken for granted.

Classical design in twenty-first century America suffers not only from the lack of adequate training of the majority of its practitioners, but also from the lack of published instructions that make the application of the classical orders easily understandable. Not since the appearance of Professor Ware's *American Vignola* over a century ago have American architects and designers had a comprehensive how-to treatise on the orders designed specifically for the modern practitioner. Robert Chitham's *The Classical Orders of Architecture*, published in America in 1985 by Rizzoli International, partly addressed this lack, but its translation of the 'best practice' ideals of British classical orders, especially Gibbs's, into a metric format limited its direct application to American design, where most building materials and ready-made components, particularly for housing, are still measured in feet and inches.

As for Gibbs, the 1937 Society of Architects' edition of his *Rules for Drawing* at least kept his orders available for a dwindling number of discerning designers. In 2000, Richard Sidwell of Monmouth House Books produced a faithful facsimile of *Rules for Drawing*, but it is intended more for the bibliophile and historian than the practitioner. Gibbs's *Book of Architecture* was reproduced in a reduced but high-quality format by Benjamin Blom in 1968, but alas, this late twentieth-century version of Gibbs's famous presentation itself now qualifies as a rare book, and rarely appears for sale. Needless to say, eighteenth-century editions of *Rules for Drawing* and *A Book of Architecture* are beyond the reach of all but the wealthiest collectors and institutions, severely limiting their ability to influence current practice.

As did James Gibbs nearly three centuries ago the revised and expanded edition of the *Classical Orders of Architecture* will help kindle a new appreciation for the foundation of the architecture of the Western World. The classical orders achieved perfection through development and adjustment over many generations. When properly proportioned and applied through time-tested formulas, they continue to inspire admiration and delight. Through his own architectural works, and especially his two books, Gibbs enabled the orders to lend special distinction to many of Britain's and America's most esteemed buildings. A renewed and enhanced understanding of the classical orders through the lens of Gibbs will further enable this ancient art to enrich our built environment.

FURTHER READING

For information on Gibbs used in this essay, I am particularly indebted to Terry Friedman's comprehensive biography, *James Gibbs,* Yale University Press, 1984.

In addition to the books by Gibbs, Palladio, Scamozzi, Swan and Vignola, cited in the text above, those works that I have used as references are as follows:

Adams, William Howard, *Jefferson's Monticello*, Abbeville Press, 1983.

Brown, Bennie, Jr. (ed.), *Buckland, Master Builder of the 18th Century*, Gunston Hall Board of Regents exhibition catalogue, 1977.

Chambers, William, *A Treatise on the Decorative Part of Civil Architecture*, third edition, Joseph Smeeton, 1791 (Dover Publications reprint, 2003).

Curl, James Stevens, *Oxford Dictionary of Architecture*, Oxford University Press, 1999.

Hafertepe, Kenneth & O'Gorman, James F. (eds), *American Architects and their Books, to 1848*, University of Massachusetts Press, 2001.

Kathrens, Michael, C., *American Splendor: The Residential Architecture of Horace Trumbauer*, Acanthus Press, 2002.

Kidder Smith, G.E., *The Beacon Guide to New England Houses of Worship*, Beacon Press, 1989.

Lane, Mills, *Architecture of the Old South, North Carolina*, The Beehive Press, 1985.

Lounsbury, Carl R., *From Statehouse to Courthouse: An Architectural History of South Carolina's Colonial Capitol and Charleston County Courthouse*, University of South Carolina Press, 2001.

O'Neal, William B. & Weeks, Christopher, *The Work of William Lawrence Bottomley in Richmond*, University Press of Virginia, 1985.

Peterson, Charles, E., *Robert Smith, Architect, Builder, Patriot 1722–1777*. The Athenaeum of Philadelphia, 2000.

Pierson, William H., Jr., *American Buildings and Their Architects: The Colonial and Neo-Classical Styles*, Anchor Books edition, 1976.

Seale, William, *The White House*, The American Institute of Architects Press, 1992.

Ware, William R., *The American Vignola*, International Textbook Company, fourth edition, 1904.

Waterman, Thomas Tileston, *The Mansions of Virginia 1706–1776*, The University of North Carolina Press, 1946.

THE 96-PART
ORDERS

PLATE 45

THE FIVE ORDERS, AFTER JAMES GIBBS

The introduction to the second edition explains the genesis of my 96-part orders. My first response to the call for a non-metric method of proportioning was to convert the 100-part scale directly to one of 96 parts, with a view to simply applying the new modular dimensions to the same set of orders as in the first edition. (One possibility was to reproduce the orders flanked by both sets of scales – on the same drawing – but I soon decided that that was a recipe for confusion.) Direct translation of the decimal values, given in the first edition, into a 96-part system produced some very awkward fractions, so it was apparent that some redrafting would be needed to round out the complicated figures involved.

Turning to James Gibbs's *Rules* rapidly solved this problem. Whether this is due to his familiarity with feet and inches, or to the underlying logic of his system of fractions, and fractions of fractions, is not clear, but certainly, as soon as I began to reconfigure his orders on the 96-part method, it became apparent that the proportions would on the whole fit very simply. As in the 100-part orders there are numerous minor elements where I have found it desirable to use fractions of whole parts, generally halves but sometimes quarters and occasionally thirds. This difficulty is mainly confined to the Doric order.

The system of dimensioning the plates follows closely that of the original metric orders. Again, there are four scales on the left-hand margin of each drawing, as in Fig. 2.

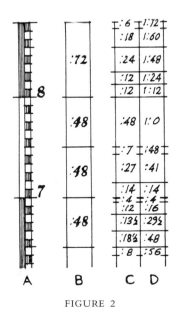

FIGURE 2

137

Scale A is the overall scale of modules (again based on the column diameter at the base of the shaft), setting each *subsequent* plate in the context of the comparative plate of the Gibbs orders (plate 45). Scale B shows the proportions of the principal divisions and sub-divisions of the order. Scale C shows the separate proportions of minor subdivisions, while Scale D repeats these as cumulative figures, always taken from an easily identifiable point, either the underside of the column base or the underside of the architrave of the entablature. In order to avoid confusion with the metric fractions of the preceding orders, fractions in the 96-part orders are *pre-fixed with a colon instead of a decimal point.*

Gibbs allows two plates to his introductory setting-out of the five orders, the first to the Tuscan and Doric, and the second to the Ionic, Corinthian and Composite. He shows them to the same overall height (including their pedestals). For the reasons already given on p.45 I have not done this here, but have used the same module dimension for all, giving them an ascending height from Tuscan to Corinthian.

Gibbs's division of the orders into two plates is as I have already mentioned significant in one way. For his 'minor' orders, Tuscan and Doric, he uses a column:entablature ratio of 4:1. For his 'major' orders, Ionic, Corinthian and Composite, he uses a 5:1 ratio. In this he follows Palladio (though allowing the Corinthian column 10 diameter to Palladio's 9½). This puts him at variance with Chambers who follows Vignola's adoption of a 4:1 ratio throughout.

The significance of this disparity is easily demonstrated. Figure 3a sketches the west portico of the church of St Martin in the Fields, London, as represented by Gibbs in the 'Approved' design of 1721, which closely resembles the finished work, although the *columns* are of the Composite order. (For a discussion of the evolution of the design, see Terry Friedman's *James Gibbs.*[22]) Figure 3b shows the same portico, adopting the column:entablature ratio advocated by Chambers. The increased overall height, and emphasis of the entablature, is quite marked, especially when the order is used in a pedimented composition.

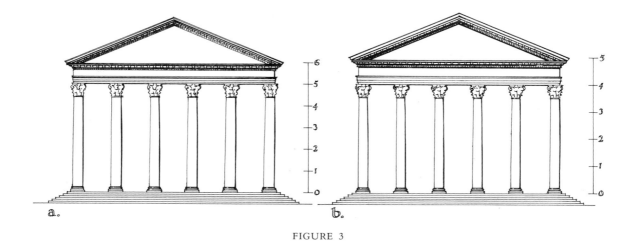

FIGURE 3

22. Terry Friedman, *James Gibbs*, Chapter IV.

138

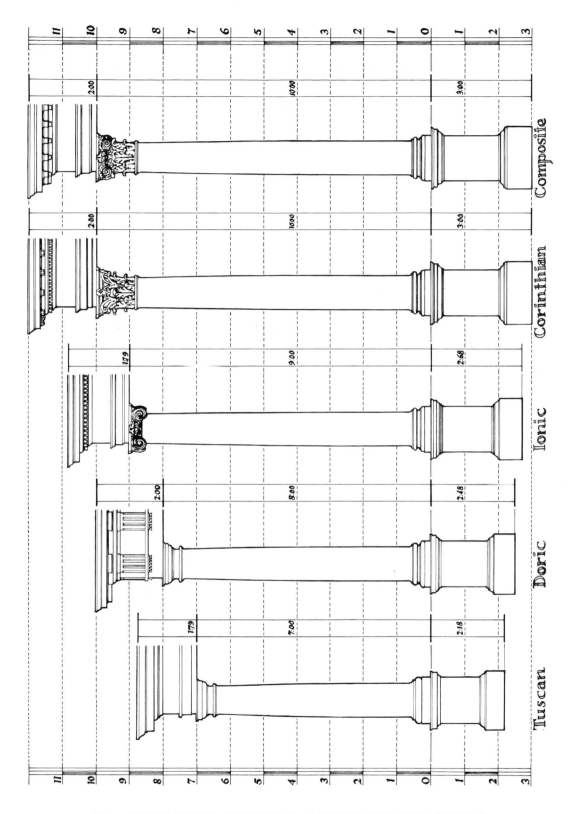

45.   THE FIVE ORDERS, AFTER JAMES GIBBS

139

THE TUSCAN ORDER

The setting-out of the Tuscan order presents no difficulties. Gibbs uses a ratio of pedestal height:column + entablature as 1:4, and the same ratio for the proportion of entablature:column. At 96 parts to 1 module this gives the following proportions:

entablature	168	(1:72)
column	672	(7:00)
pedestal	210	(2:18)

Following Gibbs's system of fractions, all but one of the major parts of column and entablature can be expressed directly as whole numbers, as can most major parts of the plinth. In order to control the relative dimensions of the capital, halves of parts are given to its ovolo and the small fillet below, and to the torus and fillet below the necking. Plate 47 shows the split architrave that Gibbs derived from Scamozzi, and here again halves of parts are necessary. There may be some reluctance to use this form of architrave in practice, lest it detracts from the simplicity of the entablature. I think Gibbs included it so as to avoid any similarity between the depth of the flat architrave and that of the frieze; it seems that to please the eye, the vertical hierarchy of an order should be such that dimensions are not repeated in adjoining elements.

Gibbs's pedestal is of course quite different in the proportion of its elements from that given in my metric orders. The principal difference is in the depth of its base, which has the merit of comfortably exceeding that of the column base. But the die is still only just over square in shape.

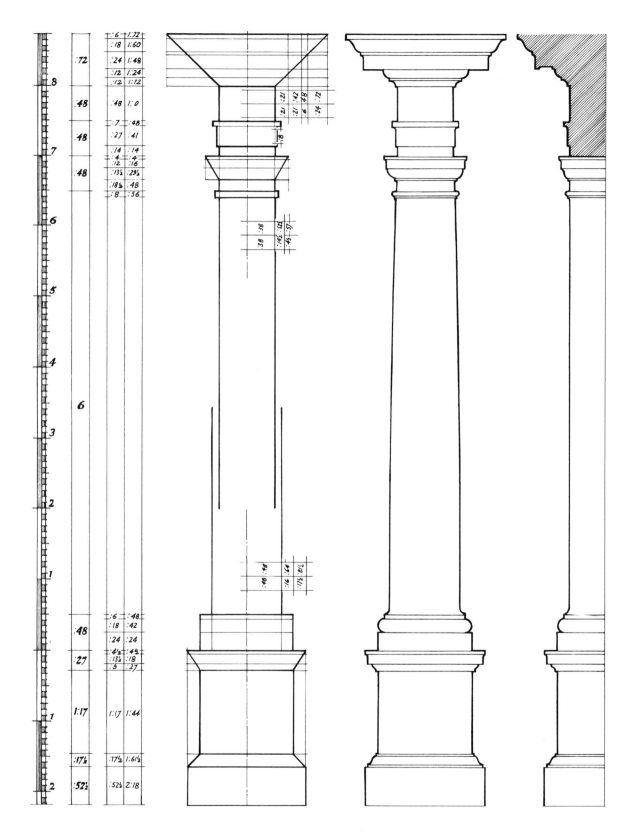

46.   THE TUSCAN ORDER

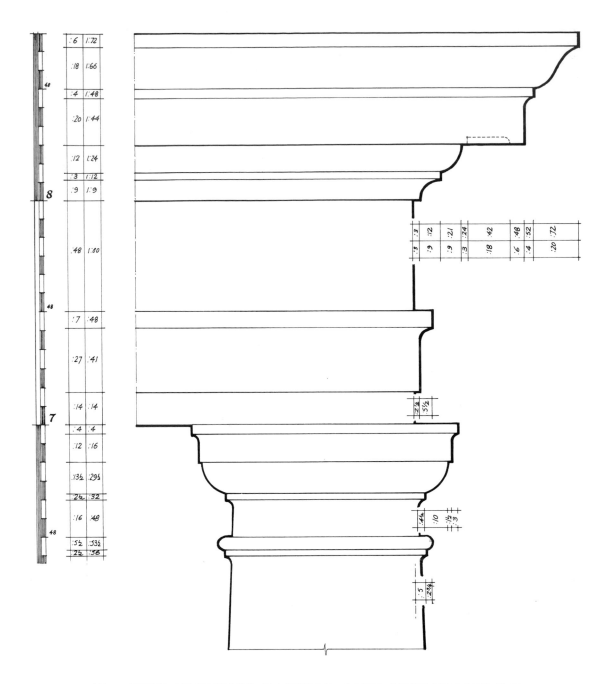

47.   THE TUSCAN CAPITAL AND ENTABLATURE

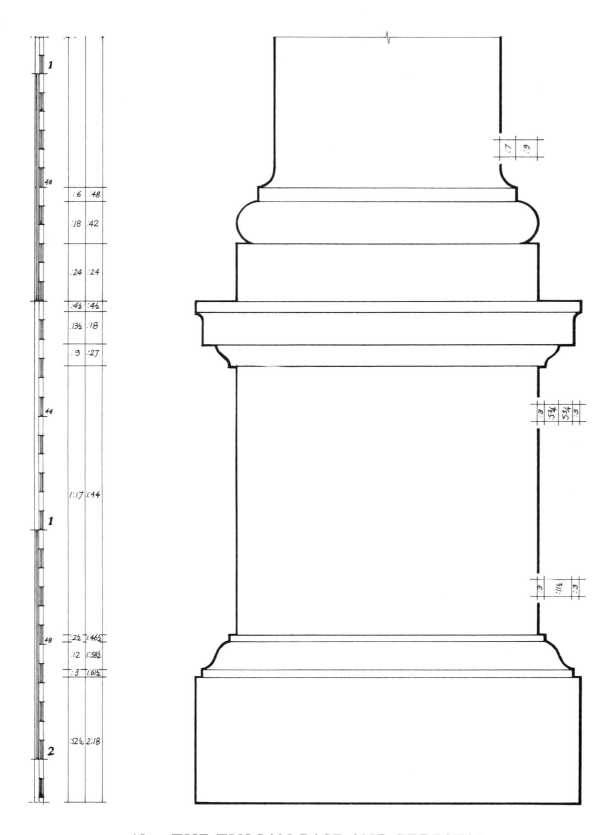

48.   THE TUSCAN BASE AND PEDESTAL

THE DORIC ORDER

Use of Gibbs's proportions for the major elements of the Doric order gives the following proportions:

entablature	192 (2:00)
column	768 (8:00)
pedestal	240 (2:48)

The major divisions of the Doric entablature can be divided into whole numbers of parts in accordance with Gibbs's system of fractions. Subdivisions of the cornice, shown in plate 50, demand the use of halves, as does the subdivision of the main elements of the pedestal.

Two further points distinguish Gibbs's detailing of the triglyph. First, the plain band above the grooves of the triglyph is given the same depth as the projecting fillet immediately above, producing a slightly heavier effect than most other interpretations. Second, the guttae beneath the taenia are drawn as quite pronounced truncated cones with their lower faces touching, a somewhat difficult form to execute satisfactorily in practice.

The 96-part and 100-part capitals are hardly distinguishable. The pedestal proportions converge, but Gibbs disposes the proportions of the plinth and cap mouldings with more subtlety than my 1:100 version, and allots more of the depth of the column base to the two tori and less to the scotia.

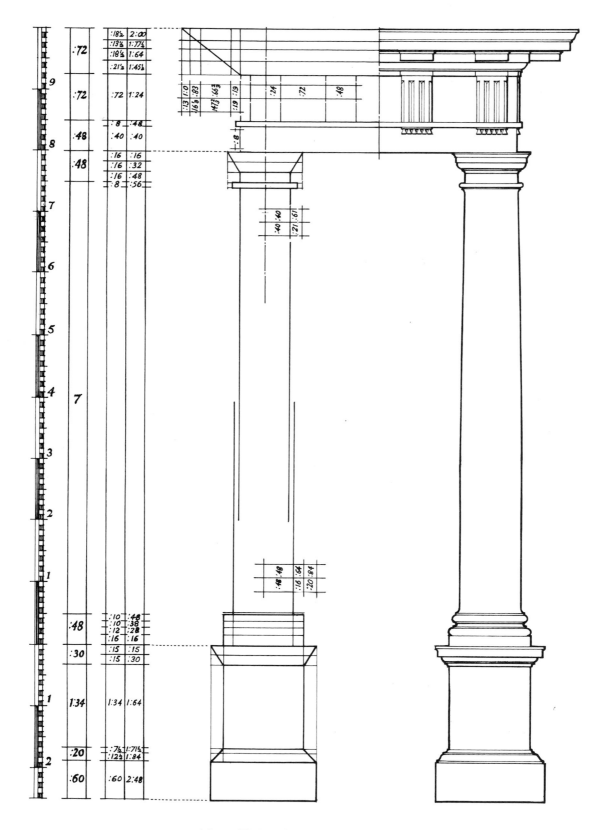

49.　THE DORIC ORDER

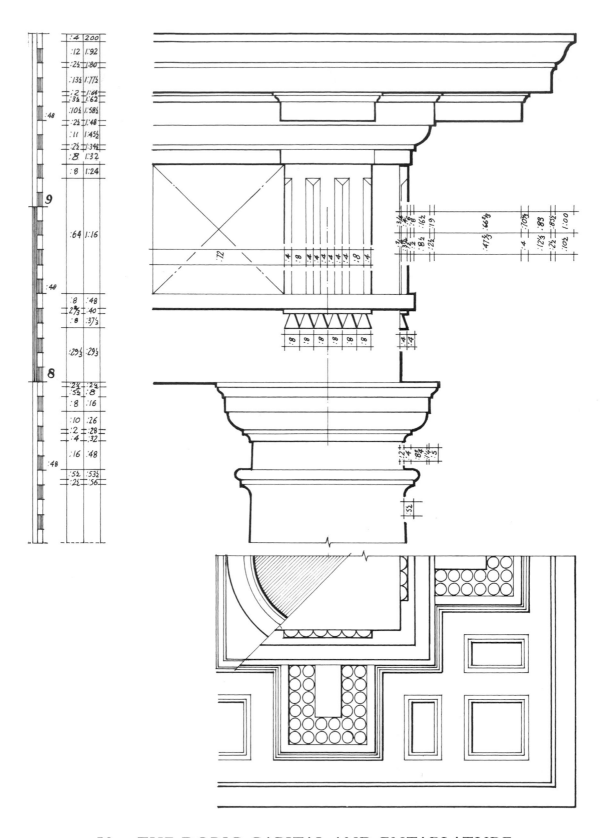

50. THE DORIC CAPITAL AND ENTABLATURE

146

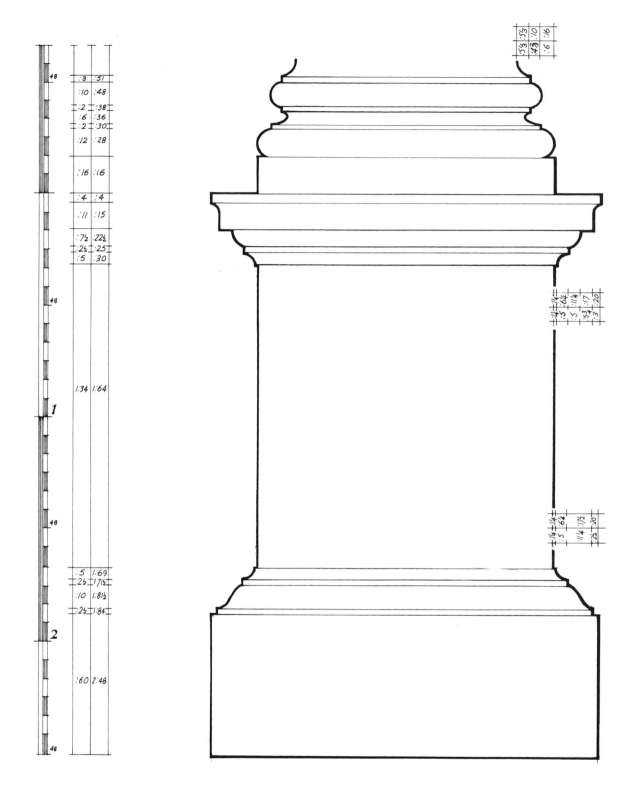

51.   THE DORIC BASE AND PEDESTAL

THE IONIC ORDER

Direct use of Gibbs's proportions for the major elements of the Ionic order produces some awkward fractions for the overall height of entablature and pedestal, so I have 'shaded' them slightly to avoid this:

	Gibbs fractions		96-part orders	
entablature	172 4/5	(1:76 4/5)	175	(1:79)
column	864	(9:00)	864	(9:00)
pedestal	259 1/5		260	(2:68)

The column is very like that of the 100-part version. I have copied the capital direct from the *Rules*, but the discrepancy between Gibbs's method for setting out the volute and that of Chambers, previously referred to, deserves notice. Indeed, I have found it necessary to substitute a new drawing of the setting out of the volute for that in the first edition (plate 18). The volute is the most difficult single element of the orders to draw, because the dimensional tolerances are so fine. The second, inner edge of the curved fillet is especially difficult. Use of the computer revealed that the method of finding the scale of the smaller square to establish the centres for the inner fillet (by similar triangles) was flawed. This error is corrected in the new edition – in my defence I can only say that the plate was copied from Chambers *Treatise* which is similarly incorrect.

To the right of the capital I have shown Gibbs's own fractional system of proportioning as I believe it clarifies the organisation of the capital's components.

Gibbs shows two forms of Ionic entablature, the first with modillions and the second with dentils. He appears to prefer the modillion form (taking it from Palladio who does not allow an alternative) as he shows it in his principal plate of the whole order. His modillions are square-ended and have hollowed soffits, rather suggesting a console form. My plates 52 and 53 give both forms. In both plates a. shows the dentil and b. the modillion form. (My own preference is for the elegance of the dentilled version.) In the drawing of the whole entablature the setting-out is shown of the pulvinated frieze, which is also shown in plate 52b.

The 96-part and 100-part bases and pedestals are virtually identical.

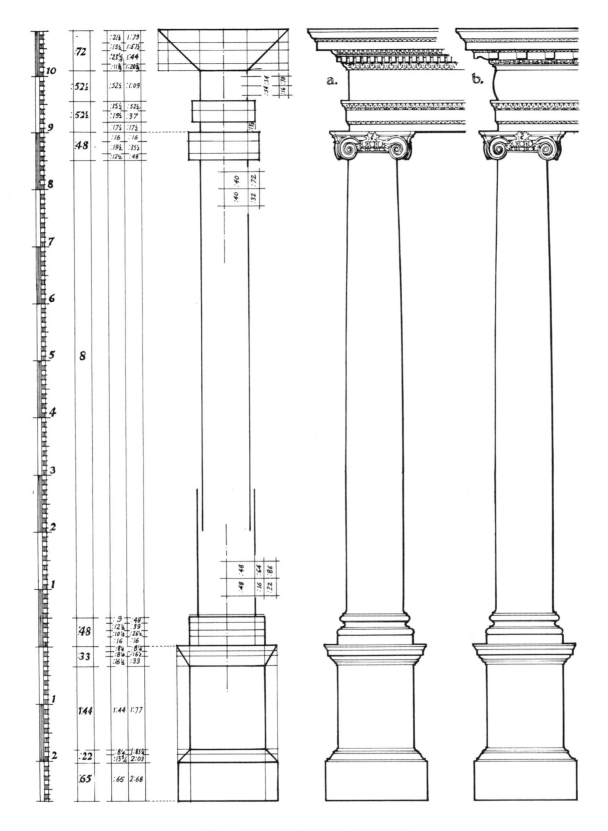

52.   THE IONIC ORDER

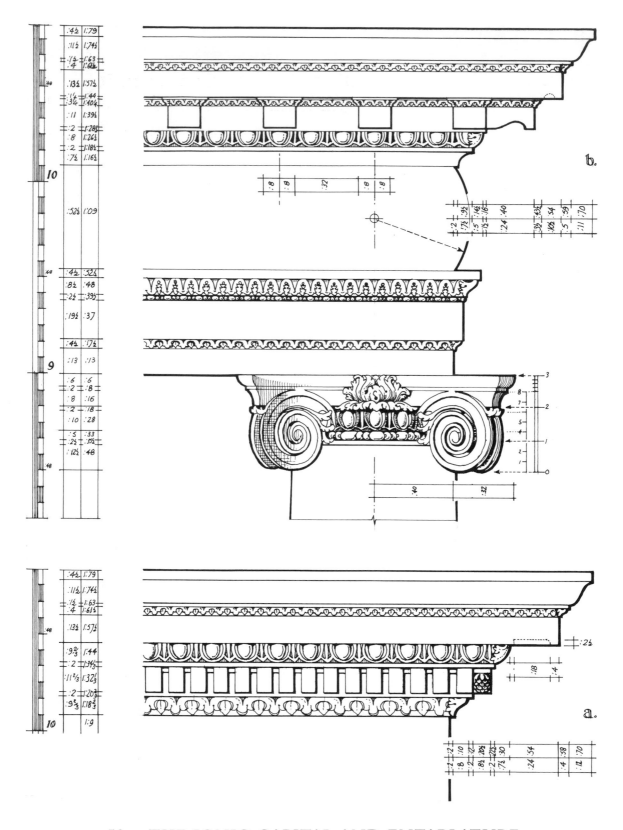

53. THE IONIC CAPITAL AND ENTABLATURE

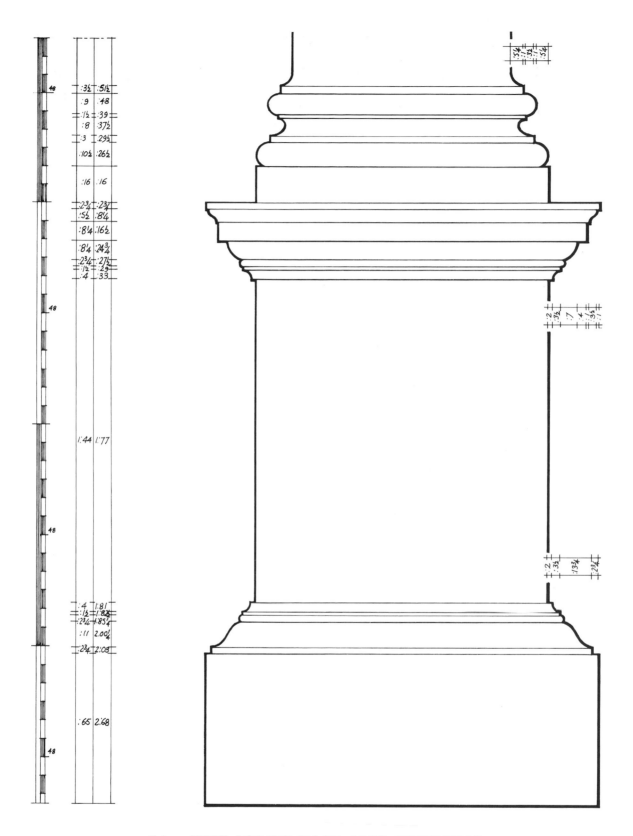

54.   THE IONIC BASE AND PEDESTAL

THE CORINTHIAN ORDER

In the Corinthian and Composite orders the rationale of Gibbs's system appears most clearly. The ratios of major elements for both orders are:

entablature	192 (2:00)
column	960 (10:00)
pedestal	288 (3:00)

A little manipulation of the elements of the entablature is however required, as Gibbs's division into 5 parts, 1½ each to architrave and frieze and 2 to cornice, clearly cannot be made using whole numbers. The comparison is as follows:

	Gibbs fractions	96-part orders
cornice	76 4/5	78
frieze	57 3/5	57
architrave	57 3/5	57

In proportioning the details of these elements, I have had to further amend Gibbs's fractions, but not to a degree that will be noticeable.

Again, the capital is derived directly from Gibbs, and his scale of fractions is shown at the right-hand side.

The column base and pedestal very closely resemble those of the 100-part order, both in overall proportions and in detail.

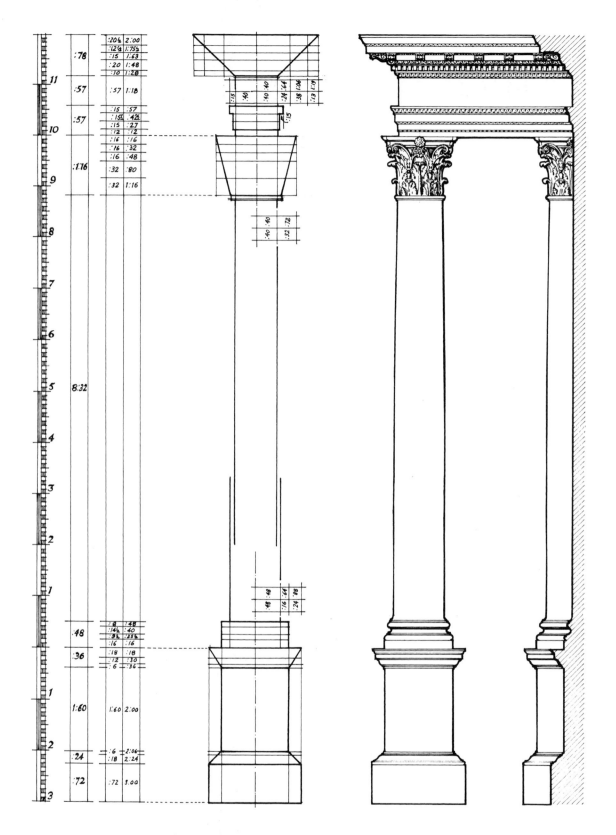

55.   THE CORINTHIAN ORDER

153

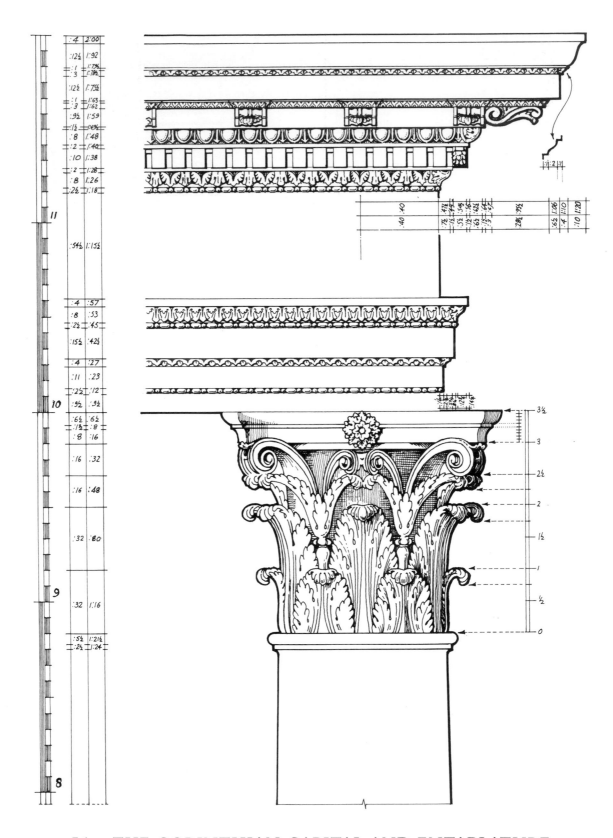

56.   THE CORINTHIAN CAPITAL AND ENTABLATURE

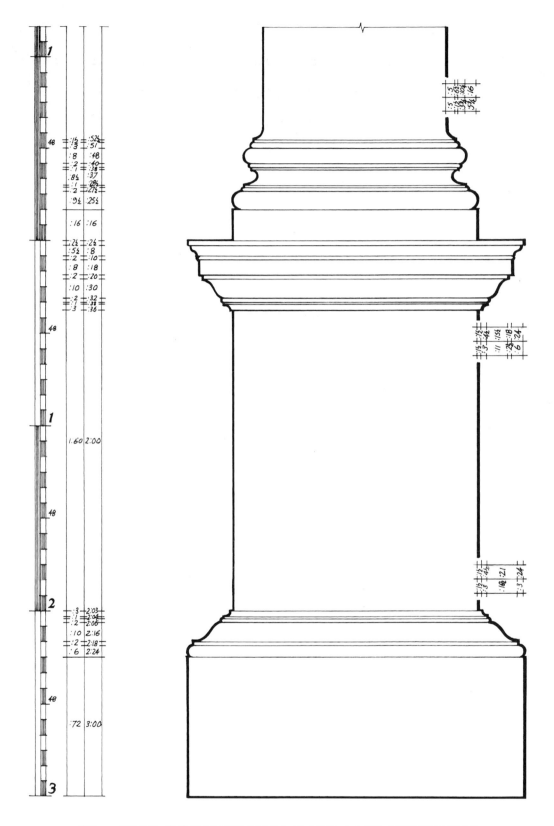

57.   THE CORINTHIAN BASE AND PEDESTAL

THE COMPOSITE ORDER

The note on the Corinthian order refers to the slight adjustment necessary to Gibbs's fractions to produce whole numbers in the division of the entablature. The Composite order follows the same pattern, and here again the column base and pedestal do not vary significantly from those of the 100-part order. The same degree of manipulation as in the Corinthian is needed to rationalise the details of architrave and cornice. In the Composite the proportions of these are somewhat coarser, with the architrave divided into two faces rather than three, and considerable emphasis on the modillions.

My capital is again taken directly from Gibbs, and again shows his system of vertical proportions, though here of course the substantial volutes occupy the space of the Corinthian's caulicoli.

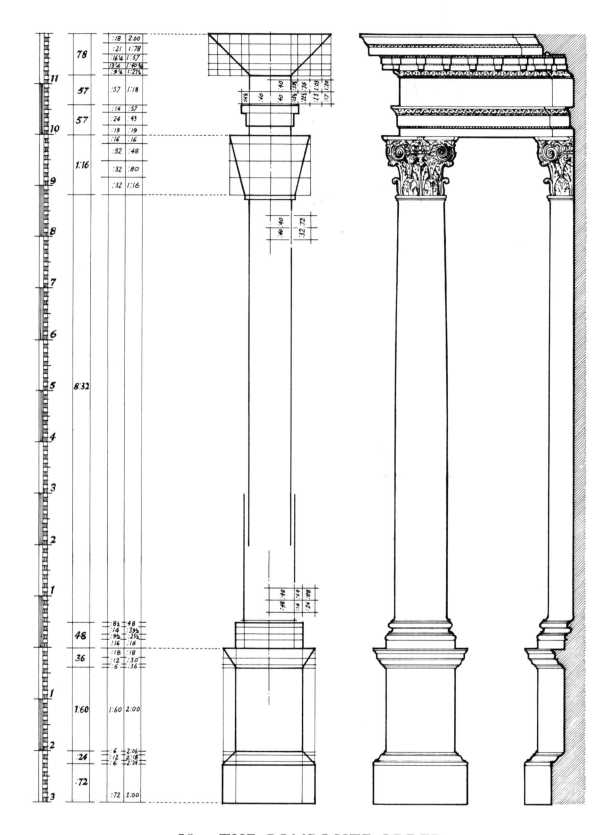

58.   THE COMPOSITE ORDER

157

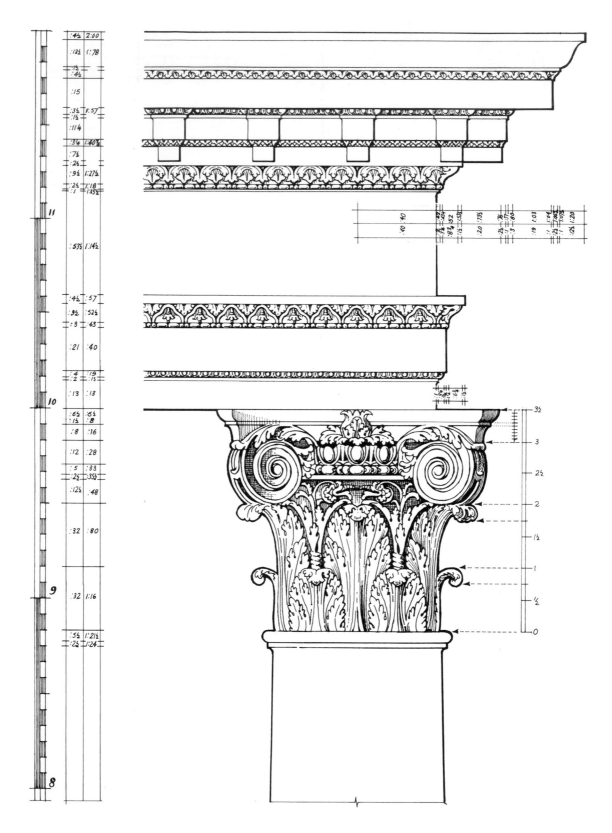

59.   THE COMPOSITE CAPITAL AND ENTABLATURE

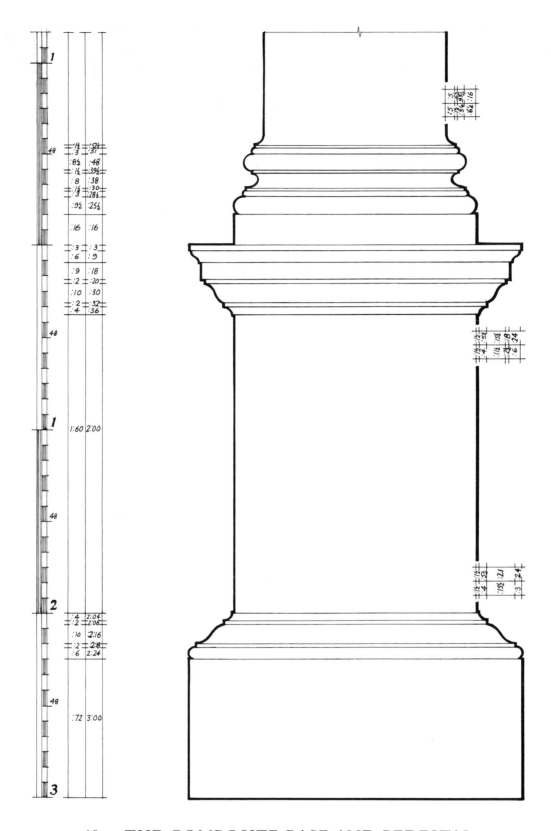

60. THE COMPOSITE BASE AND PEDESTAL

USE OF THE ORDERS

PLATE 61

THE COLUMN: DIMINUTION AND FLUTING

It was early discovered that the shaft of a column appeared more graceful if it diminished in diameter from base to capital. Most Renaissance authorities agree that this diminution should amount to one sixth of the base diameter (though Perrault allows rather less). I have adopted as a near metric equivalent of this a diameter at the head of 0.85 times the base diameter. It is not always clear at precisely what point this uppermost diameter should be measured, but I have assumed throughout that it is most logical to imagine the column length 'produced' through the capital to its junction with the entablature. Hence the breadth of the entablature is directly determined at 0.85 times the base diameter, whereas if the upper diameter is measured below the capital the dimension of the entablature is left indeterminate.

Since the ratio of upper to lower diameter is constant, the degree of curvature will be more pronounced in the shorter orders than in the longer.

Plate 61(a) takes as an example the Ionic column, as it falls between the extremes, but the method of setting out the diminution is identical for all.

Whilst the Greeks applied a curved profile to the whole length of the column, in Renaissance examples it became customary for the bottom third of the column to remain undiminished, in other words a cylindrical section, and for the upper two thirds only to be convex in profile. The curvature is so slight and subtle that it does not seem to me necessary for this division into thirds to be absolutely precise. In my drawing I have included the ovolo and bead at the head of the column (not strictly components of the shaft) as a reminder that in the Ionic order shaft and capital somewhat confusingly overlap. A further curiosity which is worth noting is that whilst the bases of all the orders are 0.5 diameters in height, only in the Tuscan is the fillet terminating the foot of the shaft included in the base.

Part (a) therefore demonstrates how to set out the curve of the diminished part of the shaft. At a point one third above the foot a semi-circle is drawn. A perpendicular dropped from the head of the shaft meets the semi-circle at A. The height of the upper part of the shaft is divided into any convenient number of equal parts (in this case seven), and the segment AB is similarly divided into equal parts, from which further perpendiculars are drawn. Where they cut the horizontal divisions of the shaft points of curvature are established, the line connecting these points being the curved profile of the shaft.

Chambers describes an alternative method, which he ascribes to Vignola. This is shown in part (b). CD and AF are the base and head semi-diameters of the shaft. An arc of radius equal to CD is inscribed with centre A, intersecting the shaft centre-line at B and the line AB is produced to meet CD produced at E. Any convenient number of lines B_1E, B_2E, B_3E etc. are drawn (not necessarily equally spaced) and lengths equal to CD measured along them to identify points A_1, A_2, A_3 etc. These points lie on the diminishing profile of the

163

shaft. The lines CD, AB are so short in relation to the column height that unless the scale of the drawing is very large it is quite difficult to establish point E with any accuracy by drawing. I calculate, however, that angle AEC, for a diminution of 0.85:1, is approximately 31°45′. Chambers illustrates a pleasing device (attributed to Blondel) for drawing a continuous curve of diminution without recourse to all this laborious construction. Unfortunately, Blondel's device only works for a specific set of column dimensions, so one would need to construct a new instrument each time a fresh order was to be drawn.

What mathematical formula governs the curves produced by these methods I cannot say. Robertson[23] states that 'the curve in Greek work is usually a continuous hyperbola, but the Romans used the parabola and other forms, and sometimes made two different curves meet'. Whilst the precise nature of the curve is clearly of consequence in setting out the shaft full size for the contractor, in preparing ordinary small scale design or record drawings I believe any smooth curve of appropriate radius is adequate.

Traditionally, draftsmen used 'railway curves' to draw arcs of great radius. The computer now performs the same function with ease.

I have deliberately used the term diminution rather than entasis to describe the curved profile of the column. It is not at all clear whether the two terms are exactly synonymous. The term entasis is derived from the Greek enteino, to stretch, and means a swelling or convexity. This conveys the impression that the greatest diameter of a column is at a height some way above its base. There is a puzzling claim, made by Cockerell in a letter to Smirke written in December 1814, to have discovered the entasis of Greek columns.[24] He cannot have been referring to simple diminution, since this was understood throughout the Renaissance. Although the measurements he describes seem somewhat ambiguous, he seems to be claiming to have found examples of columns in which the greatest diameter occurs above the base. (Robertson, on the other hand, states flatly that the profile 'in which the diameter increases for about half the height, is unknown in Greek work, at least before Roman times'.[25])

Certainly, the practice of diminishing columns towards both head and (to a lesser extent) base, has persisted, and it was particularly prevalent in the nineteenth century. It may be that the term entasis should be applied only to this variation. The two diagrams in (c) illustrate these two variations of the process of diminution. If diminution towards the base is adopted, it should be very slight; if it is overdone the effect may be somewhat comical.

Part (e) indicates the setting out of fluting, again using the Ionic shaft as an example. The Greeks used elaborate compound curves for flutes, involving great problems in the accurate execution of the work. Renaissance flutes are generally approximately semi-circular in section, and leave a fillet between adjoining flutes in the proportion of 2:6 in width (part (f)). Ionic, Corinthian and Composite shafts generally have twenty-four flutes, though the Doric may have as few as twenty. Tuscan columns are not normally fluted. Fluting may be continuous throughout the height of the shaft, or it may be confined to the diminishing part. Alternatively, the lower part of the flute may be filled with a convex cabling, as shown in part (c) which may itself be plain or enriched in the form of a rope or ribbon.

23. Robertson, *op. cit*, p. 117.

24. David Watkin, *The Life and Work of C. R. Cockerell*, p. 17.

25. Robertson, *op. cit.*, p. 116.

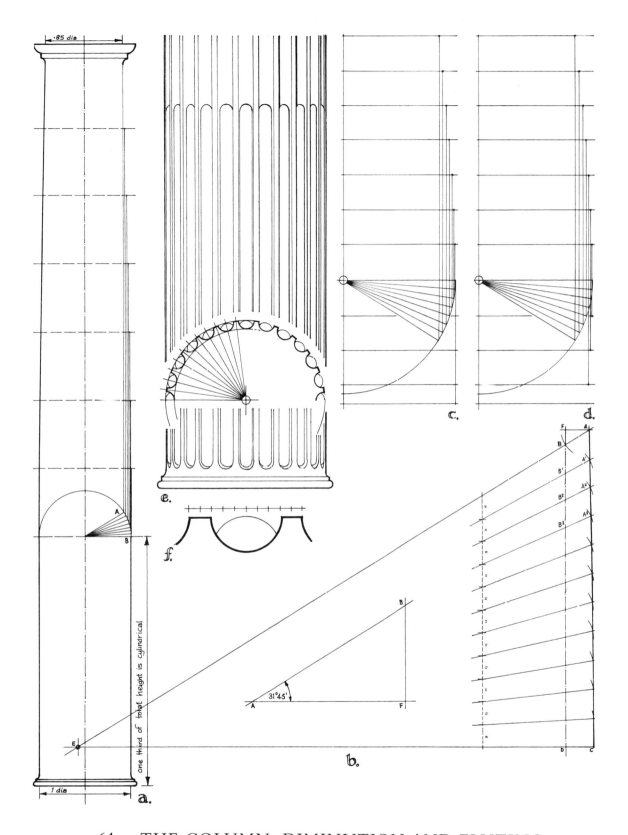

·85 dia

one third of total height is cylindrical

1 dia

a.

b.

31°45'

c.

d.

e.

f.

61.   THE COLUMN: DIMINUTION AND FLUTING

PLATE 62

INTERCOLUMNIATION I: TUSCAN AND IONIC

The spacing of columns has a considerable effect on the overall appearance of the order. A celebrated example of the sombre, claustrophobic effect of very close column spacing is the mausoleum at Castle Howard, by Hawksmoor. At the other extreme, very widely spaced columns appear to defy the structural constraints of a trabeated system of construction.

Indeed, much of the convention concerning column spacing arises from the limitations of span of stone lintels. Vitruvius cites five different spacings to which he refers in terms of intercolumniation, or the space between shafts, rather than the distance between column centres. The two narrowest are *pycnostyle* (2½ diameters between centres) and *systyle* (3 diameters). These he criticises on the grounds that they cramp the entrances to the building, and throw the wall within into deep shadow due to their close spacing. *Diastyle* (4 diameters) implies a considerable lintel span, and *araeostyle* (5 diameters) demands the use of timber in the entablature, and produces a squat appearance. The spacing favoured by Vitruvius he terms *eustyle*. This has 3¼ spacing between centres generally, but at the central openings this is increased to 4 diameters.

In practice, if the dimensions of the orders I have described in detail are adopted, the column spacings are in some instances circumscribed by the geometry of the elements of the entablature. The Tuscan and Ionic orders suffer from no restraint of this kind; the Tuscan order has no repetitive ornament to dictate the spacing, and the only repetition in the Ionic is in the dentils, which are so small in scale that they can be adjusted as necessary to suit any intercolumniation.

In the case of the Tuscan, I have shown the effect of spacing columns at 3 diameter centres (systyle), 3¼ (eustyle), 4 (diastyle) and 5 (araeostyle). I do not think, however, that it is necessary to stick rigidly to these Vitruvian spacings, and I have shown Ionic columns spaced at 2½ (pycnostyle), 3, 3½ and 4½ diameters. Spacings much above 4½ diameters are not in my view appropriate to continuous colonnades. The wider spacings are suitable for porches and aedicular elements. Where an even wider opening needs to be spanned, single columns produce a flimsy effect and alternative forms such as coupled columns, piers or arches (q.v.) must be employed.

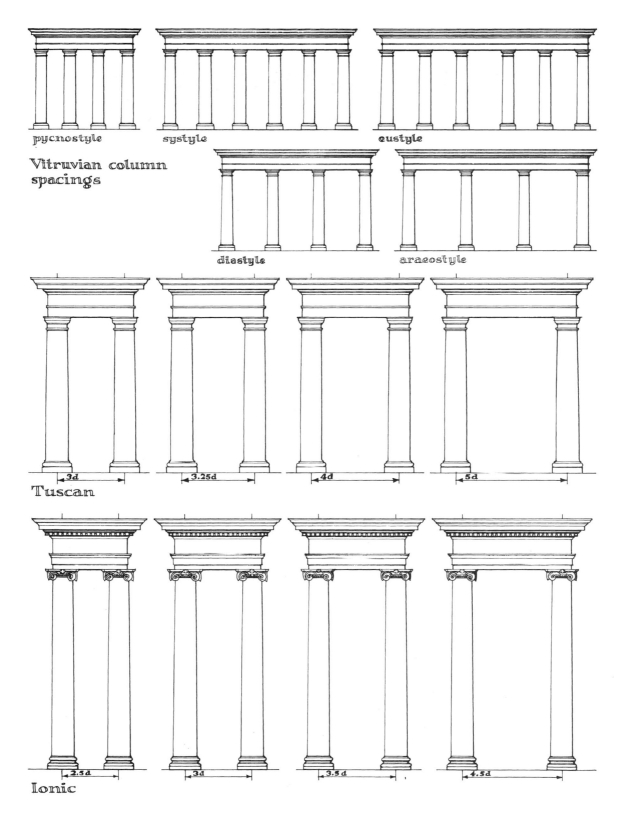

pycnostyle

systyle

eustyle

Vitruvian column spacings

diastyle

araeostyle

Tuscan

3d 3.25d 4d 5d

Ionic

2.5d 3d 3.5d 4.5d

62. INTERCOLUMNIATION I: TUSCAN AND IONIC

PLATE 63

INTERCOLUMNIATION II: DORIC, CORINTHIAN AND COMPOSITE

The spacing of Doric columns is constrained by the proportions of the elements of the frieze. The height of the frieze is 0.75 diameters, and in it square metopes alternate with triglyphs 0.5 diameters in width. This pattern thus recurs at 1.25 centres. The triglyph provides no scope for flexibility in its width, and the appearance of the whole is seriously affected if the shape of the metopes is much distorted. Since each column should have a triglyph aligned centrally in the frieze above it, this restricts the column spacings to multiples of 1.25 diameters.

At the narrowest possible spacings of 1.25 diameters, some elements of the base and capital merge, and the columns are said to be coupled. At 2.5 diameters a suitable, though somewhat close, rhythm appropriate for a continuous colonnade is generated. 3.75 diameters is still suitable for continuous repetition, but 5 diameters (araeostyle) is again only really suitable for porches etc.

The case of the Corinthian and Composite orders is a little more complicated. In both these orders the cornice is set out so that intermediate consoles or modillions align with the column centres. The proportions of the cornice and the spacing of modillions are determined by the careful proportioning of all the components and in particular the disposition of the coffers in the soffit of the corona. Gibbs in his detail plates provides the best arrangement of modillions and coffers. Unfortunately the modillion spacing set by these detail drawings does not correspond with that shown in either his general plate of the orders, nor in his diagrams of intercolumniation. Chambers consistently sets the spacing of modillions in both orders at two thirds of the column diameter, and remarks at some length on the limitations this places upon column spacing. Palladio is erratic in his modillion spacing, and I find his setting out of the corona less pleasing than that of Gibbs, with cramped margins around the coffers. Scamozzi is consistent (according to Normand) but his modillions, spaced at half the column diameter, seem crowded.

I have concluded that the best spacing for the modillions is two thirds of the column diameter, in both Corinthian and Composite orders. This restricts the column spacings to multiples of two thirds, that is, 2, $2\frac{2}{3}$, $3\frac{1}{3}$, 4, $4\frac{2}{3}$ and so on. Of these, a spacing of two produces a near-coupled column, $2\frac{2}{3}$ approximates to systyle and $3\frac{1}{3}$ to eustyle (as recommended by Chambers). Four diameters is diastyle and $4\frac{2}{3}$ approximates to araeostyle. Thus a satisfactory modillion spacing produces a worthwhile range of intercolumniations. I have shown the Composite disposed at these spacings.

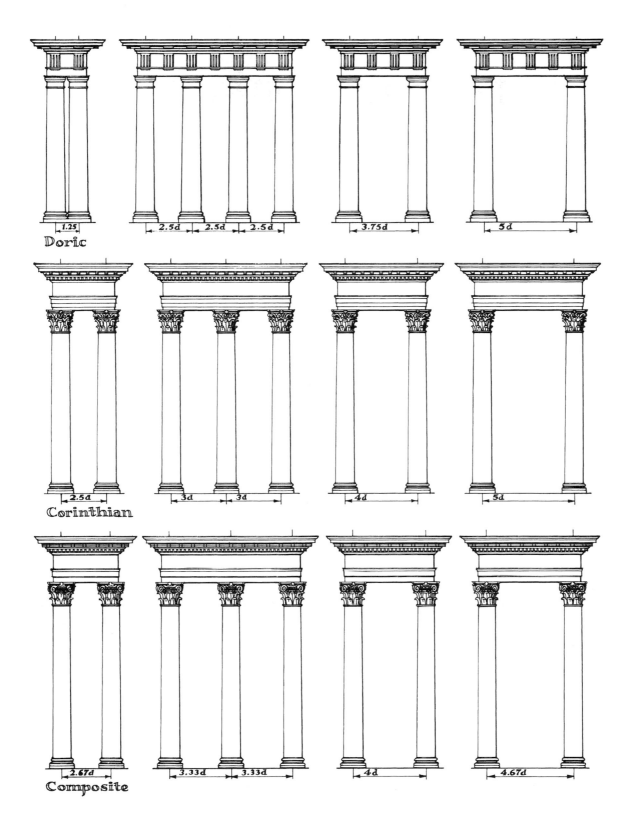

63.   INTERCOLUMNIATION II: DORIC,
CORINTHIAN AND COMPOSITE

169

The Corinthian order I show spaced at 2½, 3, 4 and 5 diameters. To achieve these intervals, the consoles must be set at ½ diameter spacing. I think it better confined to the Corinthian order with its quite slender consoles. The coarser modillions of the Composite order, set at ½ diameter centres, leave only a cramped soffit to accommodate the coffering.

The table below shows the spacing of consoles and modillions in the drawings of some principal authorities:

	Corinthian (consoles)	**Composite** (modillions)
Palladio	0.58–0.59	0.485–0.54
Scamozzi	0.5	0.5+
Chambers	0.67	0.67
Gibbs – general drawings	0.59	0.5
– details	0.65	0.54
– intercolumniation drawings	0.58	0.5

PLATE 64

ARCHES I: WITHOUT PEDESTALS

Chambers describes arches as 'proper for all apertures that require an extraordinary width'. An arch is structurally of much greater strength than a corresponding beam and column construction, and thus accommodates a greater span.

If the spacing of columns in an order exceeds a certain limit – 5 diameters between column centres is probably extreme for a colonnade of any length – the ratio of lintel length to column height becomes visually uncomfortable. Whatever the actual underlying capability of the structure, the eye is not convinced that the entablature can be maintained without either sagging or shearing at its centre. The architectural purpose of arcading, apart from introducing additional richness into the design, is to confer sufficient visual strength to permit a much wider column spacing.

Chambers sets out guidelines for the proportioning of arches. These are that the width of the piers should be between one third and two thirds of the opening width, and that the height of the opening should be about double the width. In order that the archivolt and impost should be properly proportioned to the arch, but avoid challenging the dominance of the principal order, he suggests an impost height of between one ninth and one seventh of the opening width. The least breadth of the keystone, he says, should be equal to the depth of the impost, and its height should be between 1½ times and twice its breadth.

Chambers contrives to keep his opening proportions close to his ideal by mounting the flanking columns (where no pedestal is employed) upon plinth blocks. I have omitted these in my examples and the openings of my arcades are thus perhaps squatter than he would have approved of. However, the method adopted affords a wider range of opening shapes, as the plate demonstrates.

In each case I have allowed the pilaster half the base diameter of the enclosing column. The height of the key being maintained constant through each series, the opening heights progress in steps of one diameter from the Tuscan to the Corinthian. I have allowed the Doric order to dictate the width of the whole series, since the configuration of its frieze is the least flexible. To the Doric I have allotted a column spacing of 6.25 diameters, and

I have then stepped the column spacings for the other orders in steps of one quarter of a diameter. This gives the following results:

	Width, W	**Opening** Height, H	$\dfrac{W}{H}$
Tuscan	4	6.375	1.59
Doric	4.25	7.375	1.74
Ionic	4.5	8.375	1.86
Corinthian	4.75	9.375	1.97

I have allowed an impost height and archivolt width of ½ diameter throughout. Details of impost and archivolt profiles, adapted from Gibbs, are given in plate 66.

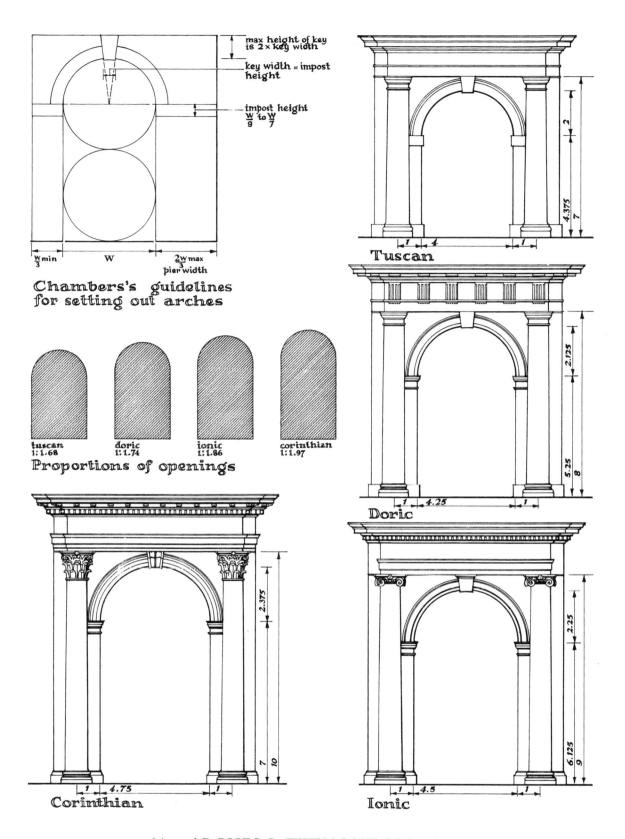

max height of key is 2 × key width

key width = impost height

impost height $\frac{W}{9}$ to $\frac{W}{7}$

$\frac{W}{3}$ min   W $\frac{2W}{3}$ max pier width

Chambers's guidelines for setting out arches

tuscan 1:1.68   doric 1:1.74   ionic 1:1.86   corinthian 1:1.97

Proportions of openings

Tuscan

1   4   1

2

4.375

7

Doric

1   4.25   1

2.125

5.25

8

Corinthian

1   4.75   1

2.375

7

10

Ionic

1   4.5   1

2.25

6.125

9

64.   ARCHES I: WITHOUT PEDESTALS

173

PLATE 65

ARCHES II:
WITH PEDESTALS

Most authorities give examples of two kinds of arcade: those where the columns are imposed on pedestals, and those where they are not. It seems to me that the addition of the pedestal to the order in this situation tends to make the order itself somewhat diminutive compared with the proportions of the arch. However, I have shown both versions.

I again allowed the Doric to dictate the dimensions for the whole series. In this instance it is necessary to allow an extra metope and triglyph to the width in order to avoid too narrow an opening. This arrangement, 5.5 diameters between column centres, produces a central triglyph over the keystone, which is less than ideal. Again, the opening widths are stepped in one quarter diameter increases through the sequence of the orders. However, because of the addition of the pedestals, the increments of height between one order and another are this time of 1.3 diameters. I was delighted to find, on drawing out these examples, that the arrangement of the Corinthian gives a height:width ratio of exactly 2:1, a pleasing fact which I celebrated by inscribing the double-circle within the opening.

	Width, W	**Opening** Height, H	$\frac{W}{H}$
Tuscan	5.25	8.1	1.54
Doric	5.5	9.4	1.71
Ionic	5.75	10.7	1.86
Corinthian	6	12	2

I have not attempted a separate drawing of the Composite order. I think for this purpose it can be regarded simply as a variation of the Corinthian. However, to each arch I have added the balustrade appropriate to the particular order, this being an opportune point at which to demonstrate the general proportions of these balustrades, whose detailed dimensions are set out in plate 67.

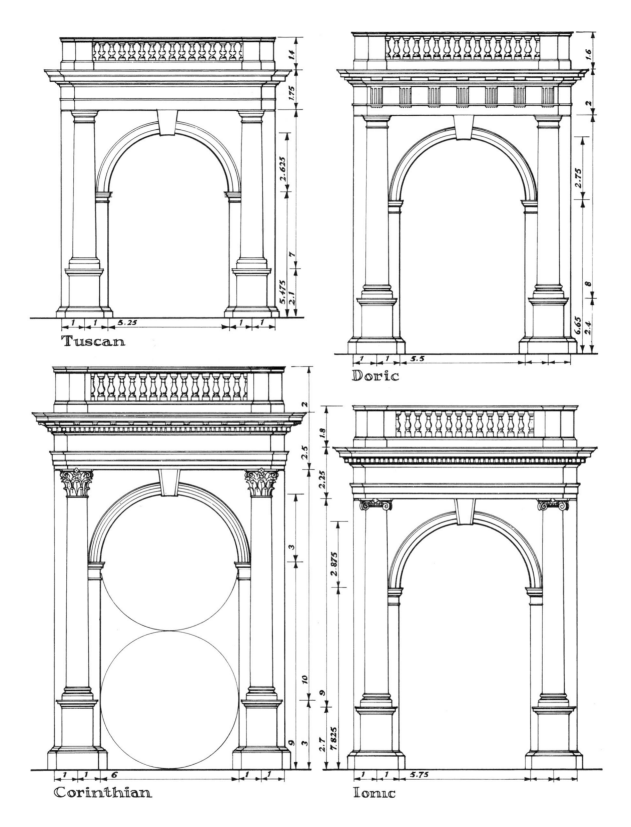

65.   ARCHES II: WITH PEDESTALS

PLATE 66

ARCHES III: DETAILS

The common shapes for arched openings are half-round, segmental, and elliptical. Chambers suggests that the spring of the arch should be somewhat raised above the impost, so that the bottom part of the curve is not lost when viewed from below. This 'stilting' of the arch should be very slight, except in the case of the segmental arch, where a fairly pronounced stilting is required to lift the segmental arch well clear of the impost. (Similarly a segmental ceiling, unless of a very pronounced curve, needs to be stilted if it is not to spring uncomfortably from a supporting cornice.)

Ellipses are not easy to set out accurately. Fraser Reekie gives four useful methods of setting out ellipses and simpler curves approximating to them.[26] One of the methods he shows involves the use of a trammel which is capable of tracing the locus of an ellipse with accuracy. I have seen a similar device used by plasterers for setting out ellipses full size. The problem remains of setting out the lines of the archivolt mouldings 'concentrically' with the basic ellipse, necessitating the use of curved templates or something similar. The fourth kind of arch I have shown, therefore, is the three-centred type, which approximates fairly closely to an elliptical form. An infinite variety of curves can be produced by varying the relative positions of the centres. I have shown a fairly common form in which the centres are arranged in an equilateral triangle, the upper two dividing the chord of the arch into three equal parts. Because it is composed of the arcs of circles, it is a great deal easier to set out than the elliptical form. And *voussoirs* are radial.

Suggested forms for the archivolt and impost are given. These are based on examples by Gibbs; the archivolts are copied directly from the architrave of the parent order (except for the Doric, which has a flat architrave), and the imposts are developed from a simple Tuscan pilaster order.

Arches which are not entirely plain may be embellished either with archivolts or with voussoirs. The archivolt, which is in the four examples in this plate, is simply an architrave stretched around the curve of the arch. Voussoirs, on the other hand, are the radiating blocks of masonry of which the structural arch is formed. Decoratively, the archivolt is probably the older form. Most Roman decorative arches were of brickwork or mass concrete, faced with stone or stucco and provided with architraves, although many examples survive of structural stone Roman arches in civil engineering works such as bridges and aqueducts.

Keystones belong more properly to arches with expressed voussoirs than to archivolts. Though there are examples of archivolted arches with keys in the work of the early Renaissance, the expressed keystone is associated much more with the voussoired arch of which it forms an essential component. The near universal projection of the keystone is an odd device, in that it suggests that the stones of the arch have been incorrectly cut or

26. R. Fraser Reekie, *Architecture and Building Graphics*, p. 44.

176

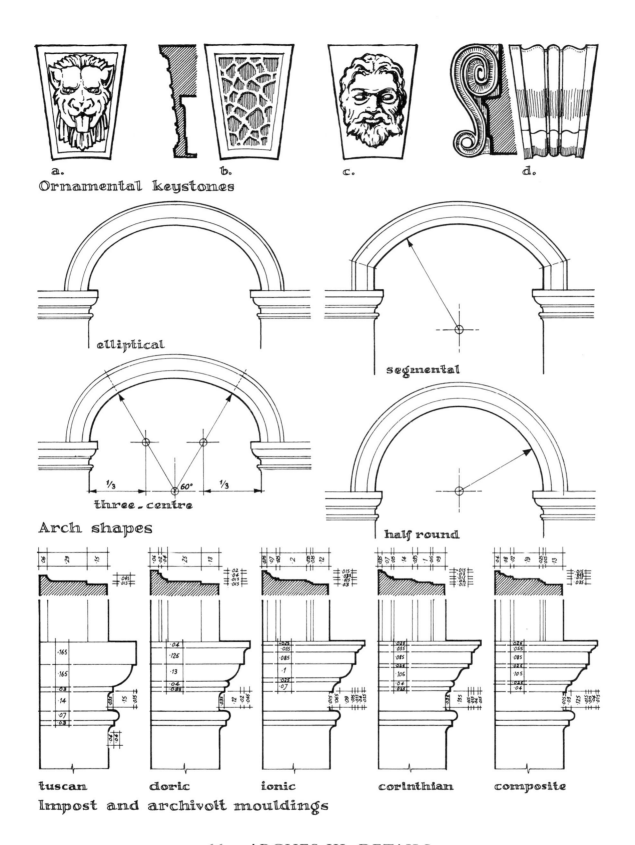

a.   b.   c.   d.

Ornamental keystones

elliptical

segmental

three-centre

half round

Arch shapes

tuscan   doric   ionic   corinthian   composite

Impost and archivolt mouldings

66.   ARCHES III: DETAILS

assembled, requiring the keystone to be driven further into the arch than it should be. It seems such a Mannerist device that it is tempting to seek to ascribe its invention to, say, Giulio Romano, but in fact many identifiably earlier examples proscribe such an attribution.

The keystone may be plain or decorated with a wide variety of ornaments, of which there is only space for a small sample. Masks of human faces or animals are common, and keystones frequently take the form of brackets or consoles in which case they are elaborately moulded on the face in a manner presumably deriving from the 'cushion' end of the Greek Ionic volute. Another common treatment I have shown is the *vermiculation* of the keystone, within a plain or moulded border.

PLATE 67

BALUSTRADES

Balustrades may be employed in a variety of circumstances. Where they serve to support a hand-rail protecting a terrace, balcony or staircase, their height and proportion are dictated by their function. The hand-rail height of 1.1 m. demanded by some modern regulations accords closely with Chambers's recommendation Of 3'0"–3'6". Ornamentally, they are commonly used to infill arched openings, or as a termination above an order. A height of about four fifths of the entablature height gives the correct proportion; in modular form this gives a convenient progression:

Tuscan	1.4 modules
Doric	1.6
Ionic	1.8
Corinthian	2.0

At the same time, since the balustrade is so familiar that it automatically conveys a specific scale, it is perhaps unwise to allow the height even of a purely ornamental balustrade to depart too far from the practical dimension of 1.1 m. For example, if the correct modular size produces a height of 0.5 m., the resulting balustrade will impart a false sense of scale to the whole order; a plain plinth or other blocking would be better than a balustrade in such circumstances.

In common with other elements of the orders, balusters and their containing plinth and hand-rail vary in elaboration from the simplest Tuscan form to the complex Corinthian, although there is no precise consensus between the various authorities regarding proportions or the degree of embellishment. For the Doric, Ionic and Corinthian orders, I have given both single and double-bellied examples. All these, I think, would normally be turned, whilst my Tuscan example is effective either in turned form or square on plan. Any square baluster should tend to be narrower than its turned counterpart, or it looks too bulky when viewed across the diagonals.

I have indicated the ruling dimensions in the plate. These may not appear to follow any easily discernible pattern, but cannot be further rationalised without blurring the distinction between the different orders. Since balustrading is somewhat tedious to set out, it is perhaps worth describing the process in a little detail. The Ionic order may be taken as typical:

1. From the base line (presumably the top of a cornice, or some similarly determinate location), draw in the horizontals representing top and bottom of hand-rail and continuous pedestal, leaving a band in this instance 1.1 in height for the balusters themselves.

2. Determine the overall length of the balustrade panel between dies. Each baluster is 0.3 in width, and the space between each 0.15. The rank of balusters is generally terminated by a half-baluster set against the die. It is therefore best to juggle the location of the edges of

the dies so that the total length of the panel is a multiple of 0.45. Divide this length by vertical lines 0.15 apart, every third line being a baluster axis.

3. Draw in the baluster abacus and plinth, to the full width of 0.3 and each 0.135 in height.

4. Establish the centres A and B, for the convex and concave parts of the baluster curve, 0.87 and 1.15 above the base line. With centre A, radius 0.15 draw the convex arc of each, cutting diagonal AB at C.

5. With centre B, radius BC, draw the concave part of each, cutting the horizontal BB at D. BD is the radius of the upper, cylindrical part of the baluster.

6. Draw in the horizontals for base and capital mouldings. The bottom of the baluster curve is located at E; thus the main proportions of the baluster are all derived from the known dimension of its greatest width. Base and capital profiles are best added empirically.

Because they involve the repetition of compound curves and mouldings to a small scale, balustrades are perhaps the most difficult element of the order to draw. I have suggested elsewhere[27] that if you have a large amount of identical balustrading to draw, it may be worth cutting your own stencil for the sake of consistency. In the inset sketch in plate 67 I have indicated successive stages in setting out a typical balustrade, in an attempt to demonstrate that the task is one of laborious repetition rather than difficult draftsmanship. The accurate setting out of the spacings and concentration on drawing, repeatedly, one part at a time, are the keys to producing a uniform result (Figure 4).

27. Chitham, *op. cit.*, p45.

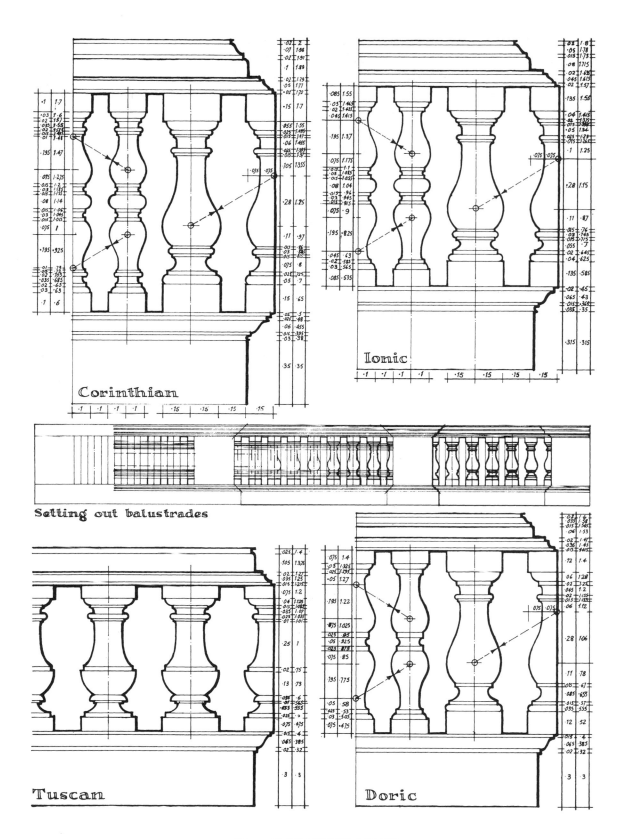

Corinthian

Ionic

Setting out balustrades

Tuscan

Doric

67. BALUSTRADES

SUPERIMPOSED ORDERS I AND II

A logical method of extending the use of the orders to embrace a building of more than one storey is the superimposition of one order upon another. The most famous ancient example is the Colosseum at Rome, which has no less than four storeys of superimposed orders. Among Renaissance architects it was Palladio who most refined the technique of superimposition, and many of his designs for villas feature 'double-decker' orders as the central element of the façade.

The Colosseum established the rule, subsequently followed fairly universally, that the superior order should always be placed over the inferior, i.e. Corinthian on Ionic, on Doric, on Tuscan. Chambers expresses it that 'the strongest should be placed lowermost', and takes the opportunity to reiterate his conviction that the Composite is inferior to the Corinthian. He also warns against the practice of omitting an order from the proper sequence, for example placing Corinthian directly above Doric. I think this over pedantic, and see no harm in omitting any of the orders, provided that the ascending order of the hierarchy of orders is maintained.

This is important as it is clearly of advantage that the more slender and elegant orders should be placed over the stockier and more solid if a top-heavy appearance is to be avoided. Equally important for the avoidance of top-heaviness is the reduction in dimensions of the ruling module of the upper order, compared with the lower. If the same lower column diameter is adopted for both, the upper order will dominate and overpower the lower to an undesirable extent, especially if pedestals are incorporated.

The question of the degree of reduction of the module of the upper order is not entirely easy to resolve. Ideally, I suppose that (assuming upper and lower columns to be concentric) no part of the upper should appear projected beyond the lower.

Thus the width of the plinth of the upper order would equal the upper diameter of the lower. Alas, this produces a scale ratio of upper to lower orders of 0.63:1 which is so radical a reduction as to make the upper order appear puny. Vitruvius recommends a reduction of one quarter from lower to upper orders, in the imitation of trees (he says), but Renaissance authorities regarded even this as too severe, and almost all adopted Scamozzi's contention that the lower diameter of the upper order should equal the upper diameter of the lower. On the decimal system I have deduced this gives a ratio of 0.85:1, which produces a pleasing proportion, as plates 68 and 69 should demonstrate.

68.   SUPERIMPOSED ORDERS I AND II

The table below gives the leading dimensions of the orders shown in the plates:

	DORIC ON TUSCAN		IONIC ON DORIC		CORINTHIAN ON IONIC	
	Without pedestal	With pedestal	Without pedestal	With pedestal	Without pedestal	With pedestal
Overall height of both orders	17.25	21.4	19.55	24.25	21.9	27.15
Upper Order						
Overall height	8.5	10.55	9.55	11.85	10.65	13.2
Entablature height	1.7	1.7	1.9	1.9	2.15	2.15
Column upper diameter	0.72	0.72	0.72	0.72	0.72	0.72
length	6.8	6.8	7.65	7.65	8.5	8.5
lower diameter	0.85	0.85	0.85	0.85	0.84	0.85
plinth width	1.15	1.15	1.15	1.15	1.15	1.15
Pedestal height		2.05		2.3		2.55
greatest width		1.5		1.55		1.55
Lower Order						
Overall height	8.75	10.85	10	12.4	11.25	13.95
Entablature height	1.75	1.75	2	2	2.25	2.25
Column upper diameter	0.85	0.85	0.85	0.85	0.85	0.85
length	7	7	8	8	9	9
lower diameter	1	1	1	1	1	1
plinth width	1.34	1.34	1.34	1.34	1.34	1.34
Pedestal height		2.1		2.4		2.7
greatest width		1.74		1.76		1.85

Plate 68 gives two examples of the superimposition of Ionic upon Doric. On the left, a single column is superimposed, without an intervening pedestal. On the right, pedestals are introduced to both superior and inferior order, and each order encloses a central arch. In both cases the module of the upper order corresponds with the diminished diameter of the lower. It can be seen that where pedestals are introduced, the pedestal of the Ionic over-sails the frieze and cornice of the Doric to an extent that may be found uncomfortable.

In plate 69, the superimposition of Doric on Tuscan and Corinthian on Ionic are examined. In each case, the setting out is in a sense a circular process. The diminished diameter of the inferior order determines the module of the superior, but because of the inherent restrictions in the entablature design of both Doric and Corinthian, the spacing of the upper columns must be resolved and that of the lower follows suit. Parts (b) and (d) demonstrate how the lack of visual balance revealed in the previous plate may be overcome to some extent in an arcade of this type. The outer columns are flanked by a responding pilaster which is allowed to depart from the rules obeyed by the columns themselves, the upper pilaster in effect inset from the line of the lower.

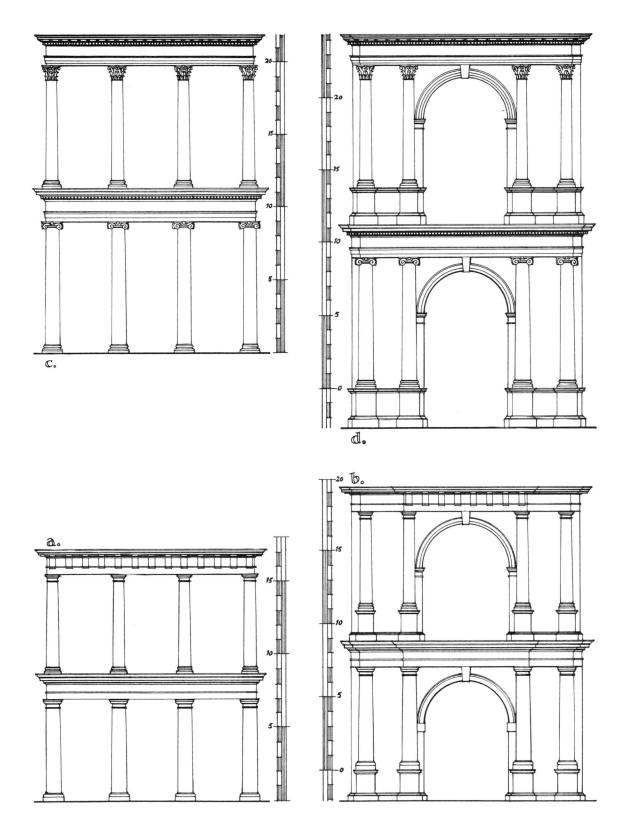

69.   SUPERIMPOSED ORDERS I AND II

ATTICS AND BASEMENTS I AND II

Whilst the superimposition of ascending orders offers an excellent way of extending their use to a multi-storey building, it will be found to be over elaborate for many purposes. The employment of attics and basements is the almost universal device by which the full potential of the orders is realised, where a lesser degree of embellishment is required. Moreover, attics and basements can be employed to give a fitting termination and balance to orders which embrace a number of storeys, termed giant orders.

Few authors seem to have attempted a rule for the proportions of either attic or basement, so I turn again to Chambers for instruction. Regarding the attic, it is his contention that it should be between one quarter and one third of the height of the order on which it is imposed. He advises that the form of the attic should be that of a pedestal, with base, die and cornice.

If such a pedestal form is to be adopted, it is proper to employ the pedestal of the appropriate (but absent) superimposed order. The table in the notes on plate 68 reveals the following ratios:

	Attic	Order	Ratio	Attic	Order	Ratio
Corinthian on Ionic	2.55	11.25	1:44	2.55	13.95	1:55
Ionic on Doric	2.3	10	1:43	2.3	12.4	1:54
Doric on Tuscan	2.05	8.75	1:43	2.05	10.85	1:53

None of these sets of proportions satisfies Chambers' recommendations; the dimensions of the pedestal will have to be somewhat elongated to fall within the range of one quarter to one third of the height of the principal order. In any case, the requirements of headroom and window sill and head heights will often call for some elongation.

The termination of any building with the crowning cyma of the cornice always seems to my eye unacceptably delicate; unless a very strong Greek flavour is sought, it generally seems better to crown the cornice with a blocking course aligning with the face of the frieze below. Where an attic is superimposed, the plinth of the attic is substituted for this plain course.

Of the basement, Chambers notes that in many Italian examples basements are of considerable height. Indeed, in Palladio's example[28] the proportions of basement height:height of principal order vary between 0.5:1 and 1.14:1. Chambers concludes that on no occasion

28. Palladio, *op. cit.*, Book 2.

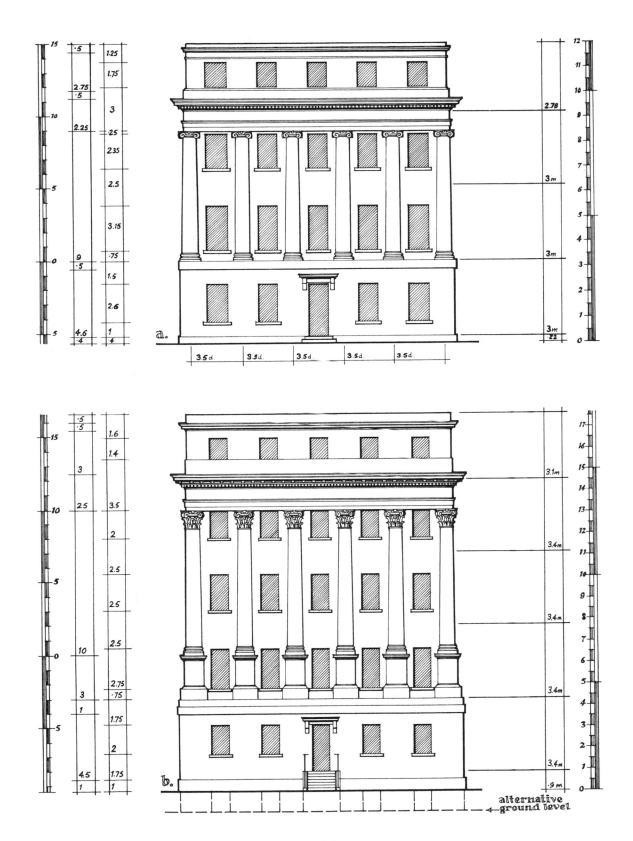

70. ATTICS AND BASEMENTS I AND II

should the basement be taller than the principal order, nor (if it is to provide accommodation) should it be less than half as high. However if the basement is used simply to raise the ground floor above ground level, it may be much lower, in the form of a continuous pedestal.

The range of combinations of basement and attic proportions must be practically unlimited, and its exploration is far beyond the scope of this book. In plates 70 and 71 I give four examples simply to indicate the extent of the range of possible combinations.

In each diagram the modular height of the components is shown on the left. This is identical for the first three diagrams. On the right is suggested an appropriate linear scale of heights in metres, and this is of course independent of the modular scale.

In plate 70, figure (a) shows a building five bays in width, with four storeys and a constant floor-to-floor height of 3 m. A giant Ionic order embraces first and second floors, the ground floor is contained within the basement and the third within the attic. It will be seen that the design is constrained by the considerable combined depth of the attic base and the main cornice below. It is only just possible, with this constraint, to combine a reasonable second floor window head height with a practical third floor sill height. It is not uncommon in this situation to elide either frieze or architrave.

Figure (b) shows the much more attenuated form of a building with five storeys over a basement, with, in this instance, a constant floor-to-floor height of 3.4 m. The giant order embraces first, second and third floors. The loftiest order available – the Composite – is employed, and a pedestal is incorporated to provide the necessary height to contain three storeys. The chief constraint is again the depth of main cornice and attic base. Two alternative basement heights are depicted. The taller of the two, half the height of order and pedestal combined, allows the basement window heads to rise above ground level, improving the lighting of the basement itself, but at the expense of making the total height of the building appear excessive. The lesser basement height, corresponding with half the height of the order only, gives a more comfortable proportion.

For ordinary use the employment of columns or pilasters upon an elevation may be thought pompous or over elaborate. In plate 71 I have therefore depicted two elevations with basements and attics where the order is implied rather than stated. Part (a) repeats precisely the modular proportion of that in plate 70. Basement and attic and Ionic principal cornice are all defined, and the window sizes and spacings are as before. The Ionic pilasters themselves are, however, omitted from this elevation, leaving a calmer and less cluttered composition. In this instance the basement is channelled to impart a greater solidity.

Finally, part (b), drawn to a larger scale, is of a three-storey elevation, the ground and first storey embraced within an implied Composite order (as is evidenced by the cornice) and the second within an attic. The whole is raised upon a basement consisting simply of a continuous rusticated pedestal.

71.   ATTICS AND BASEMENTS I AND II

189

PLATE 72

RUSTICATION

The wall surface and the surrounds of windows and doors can be treated in a variety of ways to provide a contrast to areas of plain walling. Such treatments, which are equally applicable to stone and stucco, and within limitations to brickwork, are based on the principle of emphasising or embellishing the joints between real or simulated stones. As the term rustication implies, the emphasis of the joints, often coupled with leaving the surface of the stone roughly hewn, was originally intended to suggest a rough and unsophisticated appearance by contrast to the smooth urbanity of ashlar work. More particularly, this kind of finish came to be used for basements, to give them a contrasting weight and stability beneath the more delicate workmanship of the principal order above.

Chambers sets out proposals for their proportions, stating that their height (including the joint) should not be less than one module of the superimposed order, nor much more. Remembering that Chambers's module is a semi-diameter of the column, this gives a height for each rustic course of 0.5 m. or just over. In my view, such close spacing gives a rather cramped scale to a basement, and a height of about 0.75 is preferable. A height of 1 m is worth considering when a really massive appearance in the basement is desired.

As to the proportion of the joints, these vary widely depending on their profile. Chambers suggests as suitable from one tenth to one eighth for square sinkings, but as much as a quarter to a third for chamfered joints, whilst Gibbs sets the joint size as one eighth of the total height of each course, whether chamfered or not.

Plate 72 shows a number of applications of rustication. Part (a) is a semi-circular arch with vermiculated voussoirs set in plain channelled walling, that is, with the perpends omitted so that the wall is divided into a series of simple horizontal strips.

In (b), a segmental arch with an elongated key is set in rusticated walling with chamfered joints; note that the arch springs from the mid-height of a course rather than from a joint, avoiding a slightly awkward junction of jointing at the spring. Part (c) is a variation showing an opening with a flat arch, while (d) shows a number of joint profiles of increasing elaboration. Note the convention in both these examples that the keystone projects below the general line of the arch, giving the visual impression that it is firmly wedging the whole structure together.

The use of rustication is often confined to the corners of buildings, where the raised stones are known as *quoins*. The stone proportions are alternately 4:2 and 3:2 in my two examples, each of which also shows a possible crowning cornice for rusticated work. The

72. RUSTICATION

191

lower example is particularly suitable for the termination of a basement, where the projection of the cornice should be kept to a minimum in order not to detract from the proportions of the order above.

Parts (f) and (g) show rather more specialised use of rustication. (f) is a 'blocked' column, in this instance Ionic. Each block is 1 m in height, its width corresponding with that of the column plinth. (g) shows a door surround similarly 'blocked', an example taken from Gibbs, after whom this device is often known.

PLATE 73

PEDIMENTS

A pediment is originally the expressed gable-end of a pitched roof, finished by means of raked cornices along its inclined edges. In the early use of the orders for the enclosure of predominantly rectangular temples, each narrow end was therefore pedimented. Subsequently the pediment, whilst retaining its original function, also developed into a purely decorative feature, frequently taking on a miniature or aedicular form as the termination of a door or window surround.

It follows that a wide variety of pitches may be suitable for pediments. The roofs of Greek and Roman temple-buildings were generally very flat pitched, seldom rising above about 17½° from the horizontal, Greek pitches being on the whole a shade flatter than Roman. Indeed, the adoption of a very flat pitch to a pediment is one method of imparting a neo-Greek flavour to a design. Aedicular pediments are normally somewhat steeper, partly through necessity, for the proportion of the moulded cornice to the tympanum is such that in aedicular form the latter all but disappears if the raking cornices are not well pitched up. In early English Renaissance work pitches, especially of dormer pediments, exceed 45°; from this peak they gradually subside until the onset of the neo-classical.

Plate 73, parts (a)–(e) show a series of variations upon the same type of pediment, all set at a pitch of 22½°. Part (a) represents a standard triangular pediment above, say, a doorcase of Tuscan pilasters. *It is to be noted that the crowning cyma of the cornice is used on the raking cornices only and not on the horizontal cornice below the tympanum.* The small fillet terminating the corona is continuous, linking the raking and horizontal cornices. The section of all the mouldings beneath this on the horizontal cornice is reproduced, on the skew, on the raking cornices, so that it follows that frieze and tympanum are in the same plane.

There seems to be no consensus regarding the terminology of 'broken' and 'open' cornices. Finding it easy to remember that things are often 'opened up' or 'broken down', I define the following figures accordingly. Part (b) is a form of broken pediment, where the horizontal cornice breaks back between the pilasters, whilst (c) is both broken and open, in that both horizontal and raking cornices break back in the centre. Part (d) is a fully broken pediment; here the centre part of the horizontal cornice is omitted altogether in order to allow a semi-circular arch rising from imposts to rise into and occupy the tympanum. Finally, (e) is a properly open pediment, with most of the raked cornices, and the enclosed tympanum, omitted.

When the order to be pedimented includes cornice embellishments such as dentils or consoles, the problem arises of how they are to be treated in the raking cornice. Part (f) shows the solution. The embellishments, in this instance dentils, appear in the raking cornice directly over their counterparts in the horizontal; it is to be noted that their sides remain vertical, so that they assume the shape of a parallelogram in elevation.

An alternative form for the pediment is segmental; I have shown this form in part (g), over an Ionic entablature with a pulvinated frieze. Here again, embellishments such as dentils are vertical sided. It is quite common, where windows are decorated for example, for triangular and segmental pediments to alternate. Part (g) indicates how the segmental pediment may be drawn to the same height as a corresponding triangular one. Point a, the apex of the fillet crowning the corona, is joined to point b, line cd is constructed at right angles to the mid-point of ab. cd extended cuts the centre line at e which is the centre for the segmental cornice.

Part (h) is an alternate form of segmental cornice, open in form and with the tympanum pierced by a three-centred curve. This, and the many more elaborate pediment forms which are available, is probably more suited to small-scale applications, for example furniture and clocks, than to large-scale architectural use. Part (j) shows a common variant especially suitable to domestic porches. Here, the segment has become a semi-circle and it springs not from the extremities of the horizontal cornice, but from about the centre line of the flanking brackets. The guiding principles remain the same, however, the fillet over the corona being again the sole continuous member. The final sketch, (k), shows typical proportions for further ornaments upon the pediment. The flanking urns rest on vestigial blocking pieces which align with the frieze, whilst the central statue has a similar base which rises just clear of the apex of the cyma. Chambers states that statues imposed upon balustrading should not exceed one quarter of the order in height, but he gives no corresponding regulation for statuary upon a pediment.

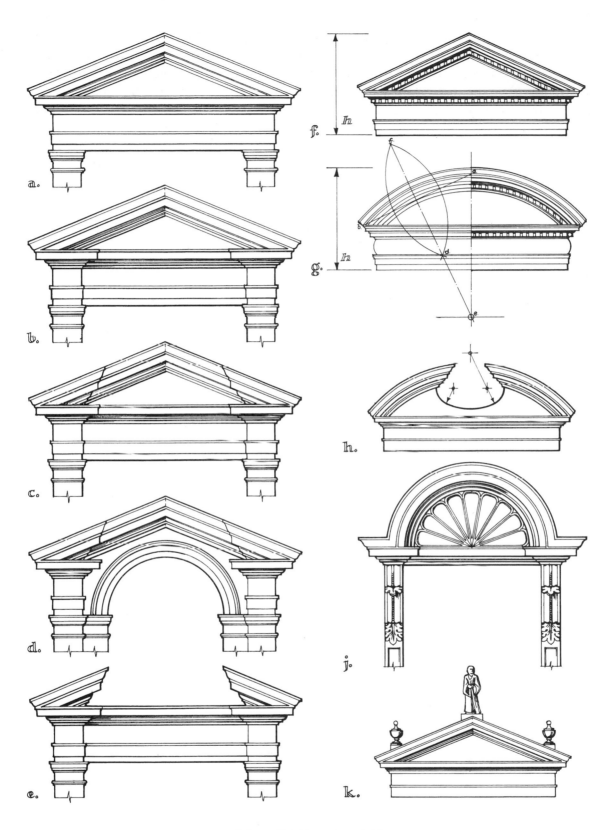

73.　PEDIMENTS

PLATE 74

DOORS AND WINDOWS I

The subject of forming door and window openings in a classical manner is such a broad one that it may be said to go considerably beyond the scope of this book, in the sense that the book is deliberately limited to an account of the vocabulary of the orders, rather than concerning itself with how they are to be employed in the design of buildings. The design of doorways is properly a part of this wider subject; I have simply taken space here for a couple of conventional domestic door surrounds, and for some windows of a standard type.

Figures (a) and (b) show two kinds of domestic doorcase. Each is based on a front door width of 5 diameters; that to (a) has a door 11 diameters in height, set in flanking pilasters supporting a semi-circular arch containing a fanlight, in turn flanked by panelled pilasters carrying curved brackets which support a broken pediment. Part (b) shows an alternative form within the same overall dimensions. Here, the door itself is 10 diameters high (having a proportion of 2:1) and six- rather than eight-panelled. The door and its rectangular fanlight are contained by a full Corinthian order on plain block pedestals, supporting a full entablature with broken pediment.

Figures (c) and (d) show two forms of Venetian window (alternatively known as Serlian or Palladian windows). In this example both are based on the Doric order, but any order may be adopted. The window consists essentially of a central light with a semi-circular head, flanked by minor side lights; in (c) this is the whole of the composition, but in (d) the window is further elaborated by its being placed in a round-headed recess which repeats the curve of the central light. Any desired degree of elaboration may be adopted, provided the overall form, with its rounded centre, is maintained. The frame may be a conventional sash form of timber, set into brickwork with a continuous gauged brick arch substituted for the entablature.

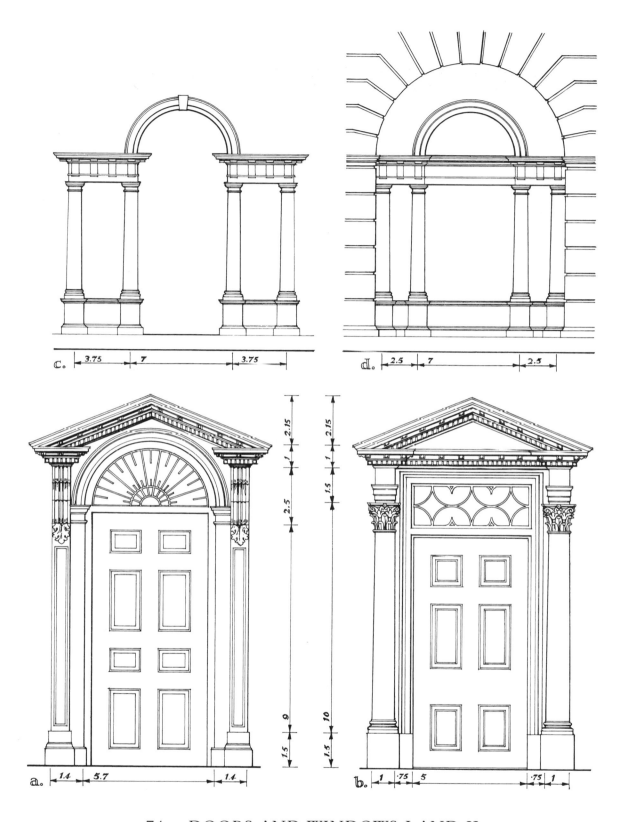

74. DOORS AND WINDOWS I AND II

PLATE 75

DOORS AND WINDOWS II

This plate suggests how the degree of enrichment of a window surround may be varied according to the location of the window on the elevation, thus introducing a hierarchy into the fenestration. It will be seen that various elements may be either present or absent from the ensemble and may be decorated to a greater or lesser extent.

The simplest window opening has no decoration of any form – strictly speaking it does not even require a sill. In window (a) a plain moulded architrave is introduced; this is the simplest possible form of enrichment, but it may be elaborated by giving it ears, as in (e), stepping the ears, as in (g), or terminating them in volutes, as in (h). The sill may be plain, or it may be moulded, as in (c). It may be supported by brackets, as in (d), and the contained space within the brackets panelled, as in (m).

Over the window a cornice may be placed, as in (b). This may be plain or it may be raised above a frieze, as in (f). Furthermore, it may be pedimented, with a triangular pediment (d) or a segmental pediment (g), and cornice alone (k) or cornice and pediment together (i) may be supported by brackets. Finally, the window opening may take a completely aedicular form, as in (m), with a full order of colonettes arising from the bracketed sill and supporting a complete pedimented entablature.

The left-hand margin of the plate shows a series of four windows divided by glazing bars. The overall proportions of the sequence are 1×1, ($1 \times \sqrt{2}$, $1 \times \sqrt{3}$) and 1×2 respectively, which are all popular eighteenth-century window proportions. In each case the window is divided horizontally into three; the vertical division is intended to produce the most pleasing proportion of subdivision. It can be seen that this minor proportion cannot be maintained constant throughout the whole range of different sized windows. An elegant alternative would be to determine the minor 'module' first and then size all the windows in an elevation in multiples of this module – they will then of course depart somewhat from the favourite overall proportions cited here.

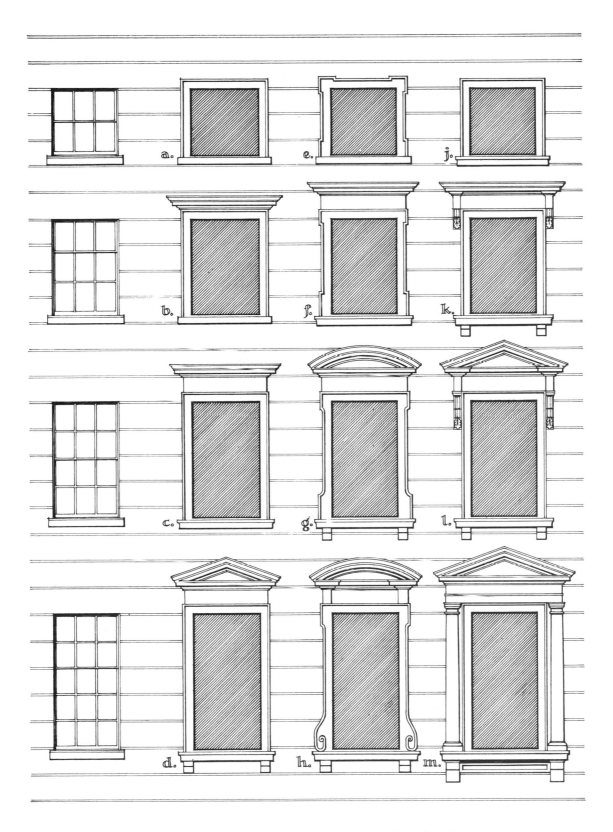

75.   DOORS AND WINDOWS I AND II

PLATE 76

MOULDINGS AND THEIR ENRICHMENT

Chambers includes a plate mainly devoted to what he terms the regular mouldings, of which he identifies eight kinds: the ovolo (quarter-round convex), the talon, more familiarly known as the cyma reversa, the cyma, the cavetto (quarter-round concave), the torus (half-round convex), the astragal (a miniature torus or bead), the scotia (a concave moulding of compound radius) and the fillet, a square projecting bead. Plate 76 displays a number of possible methods of enriching these mouldings, and the fascia or corona.[29]

All these mouldings, including many of their enriched forms, are present in the Greek orders. Banister Fletcher has a plate 30 comparing Greek and Roman forms which suggests that generally the Greek forms were constructed from more complex curves, and were thus more sensitive than their Roman counterparts, let alone the Renaissance examples derived from them.

I have indicated in the plate all these common mouldings, and have shown how they are constructed. All mouldings are designed to provide a curved profile between two fixed points, generally the termination of adjoining fillets. The angle and distance between these two points varies, not least between the different orders in which they occur. The constructions shown apply for any reasonable juxtaposition of fixed points. Most are self-explanatory and all but the *scotia* are achieved with compasses only, without the need for any measuring. It should be emphasised that there is some flexibility in the way each may be drawn. The degree of curvature depends on the circumstances in which a moulding is used, on the scale of the order of which it is part and on its location relative to the position of the observer. The mouldings forming the cornice of a giant order in a lofty exterior location can afford to be more robustly rounded than those embellishing the rim of a domestic table. On the whole, perhaps, curves should be exaggerated rather than understated. As an illustration I give two examples of the *cyma reversa*, one considerably bolder than the other in curvature but at the same time restricted in projection.

The only moulding of any complexity is the *scotia*. Gibbs and Chambers both show methods of setting this out graphically. Both, however, only work for particular locations of the containing fillets. I have been unable to establish a method using compasses only which satisfies all reasonable end-conditions without fudging. Recourse to an ellipse for the lower curve overcomes this problem, the upper curve being simply the quadrant of a circle of a radius of one third of the height between the fillets.

A few more general points may be noted. First, the curves of mouldings are not normally finished tangentially to the horizontal. The ovolo and the cavetto are both somewhat

---

29. Chambers, *op. cit.*, p. 27.

30. Sir Banister Fletcher, *A History of Architecture and the Comparative Method*, p. 125.

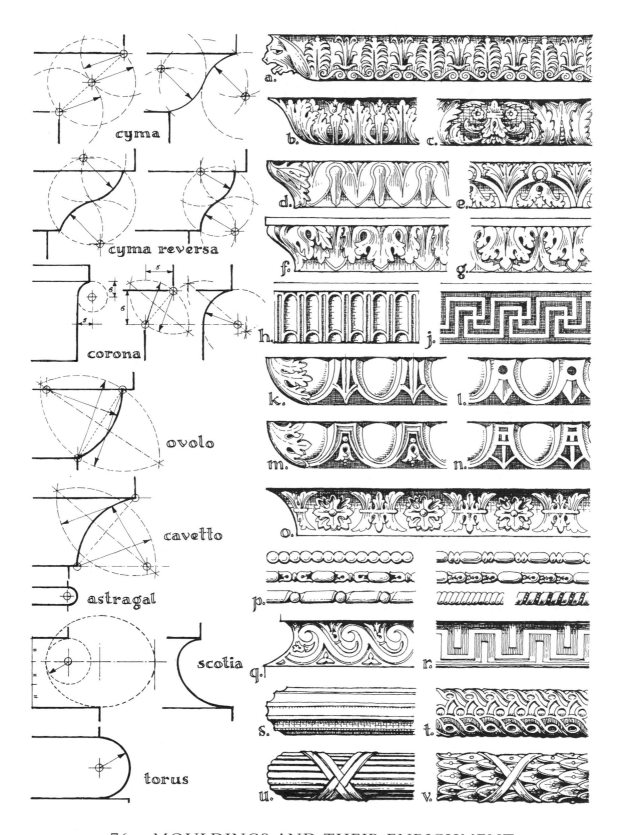

cyma

cyma reversa

corona

ovolo

cavetto

astragal

scotia

torus

76.   MOULDINGS AND THEIR ENRICHMENT

less than a quadrant, for example, and the junction of the scotia, may make a pronounced angle with the adjoining fillet below. Thus a certain subtlety may be maintained, as well as providing the necessary weathering of external mouldings.

The sequence of mouldings is fairly well established, though a glance at the comparative plates shows that considerable variations have been adopted in the past. Generally, it seems to make the best sense to succeed a concave with a convex moulding; in most cases it is obvious whether or not a plain fillet is needed between two adjacent mouldings. I do not myself much care for the juxtaposition of successive convex mouldings, for example in Scamozzi's Tuscan capital.

In the right-hand half of the plate I have sketched a number of enrichments appropriate to each of the mouldings shown, though there is of course no limit to the variety of ornament that invention can contrive. Little comment is needed. I have shown three possible enrichments of the cyma, (a) a Greek anthemion and palmette, and (b) and (c) from Renaissance examples. It is worth bearing in mind that the crowning cyma of an exterior order is, however, very seldom enriched, presumably because its exposed position would make such work peculiarly prone to erosion. (d) to (g) are enrichments for the cyma reversa, the leaf and tongue form again of Greek derivation, the remainder Roman.

The corona, again, is commonly left undecorated; (h) and (j) are typical of the geometrical designs appropriate to its flat surface, the latter a key pattern. The egg and tongue, or egg and dart, in various forms – (k) to (n) – is almost universally adopted for the ovolo, whilst the cavetto may be adorned with complex leaf forms, as in (o). Any amount of combinations of beads, ribbons, ropes, leaves and so on can be adopted for the astragal (p), whilst at (q) and (r) I show a Vitruvian scroll and a fret pattern for the scotia, again, because of its considerable convexity a difficult moulding to find suitable forms for. The torus offers much more scope. The horizontal fluting(s) is reminiscent of the Attic base, whilst reeds and laurel, bound with ribbons, may be used – (u) and (v). The Guilloche (t), a complex interlaced form, occurs also in the flat, upon the borders and margins of coffered ceilings. The best source of inspiration for the enrichment of mouldings (or of anything else, for that matter) that I have come across is Meyer's *A Handbook of Ornament*.

Fillets, the small vertical bands which separate and relieve mouldings, should always be left unadorned.

PLATE 77

CHARACTERISTICS OF CLASSICISM

Throughout the book I have endeavoured to restrict myself to a straightforward examination of the five orders, without being lured into the infinitely broader and more difficult subject of classical design. The trouble with treatises on the orders is their tendency to sag towards the end. Having dealt with the major issues, the design of the principal orders themselves, they are brought to a conclusion in a sort of mopping-up operation, with dissertations on doors and windows, mouldings and minutiae. Finding myself in this almost unavoidable situation, I trust the reader will allow me to round off the book with rather more of a flourish, indulging in a few thoughts on the essential characteristics of classical architecture.

Summerson begins *The Classical Language of Architecture* by discussing what constitutes classicism. He defines it, firstly, as architecture 'whose decorative elements derive directly or indirectly from the architectural vocabulary of the ancient world'. But he goes on to discuss a much broader definition of classical architecture as an architecture dependent on the harmony of its parts, this harmony residing especially in the proportions of the orders.[31] He makes the important point, however, that whatever its system of proportion, a building cannot be regarded as classical which does not exhibit all or some of the recognisable features of the orders. In this plate, I wish to examine briefly the other side of this coin. For whilst a building stripped of all classical form cannot truly be regarded as classical, no building can be made classical by simply dressing it with elements borrowed from the orders. There are certain characteristics of layout and composition which are essential to classicism in building design. In the plate, I have attempted to illustrate in diagrammatic form four characteristics which may be expected to be expressed or implied in any classical building.

1. SYMMETRY

All classical buildings exhibit symmetry in both elevation and plan. In the purest examples the right half of an elevation is simply a mirror image of the left. This is not always possible to achieve, nor always appropriate, but a high degree of symmetry is always likely to exist. This extends both to the overall composition of an elevation, and to its component elements. If a building is terminated in a projecting wing or pavilion, for example, this element of the whole composition is itself likely to carry a symmetrical pattern of fenestration and architectural embellishment.

31. Summerson, *op. cit.*, plate 61.

Whilst a study of the orders is in a sense not concerned with plan form, it is worth noting in this context that symmetry in classical building rules the plan as well as the elevation; to a great extent classical plans depend for their effect on axiality. One of the chief joys of Renaissance buildings is the manner in which axes are exploited to obtain sequential views, and symmetry and axiality are maintained in complex plans with a multiplicity of rooms of different shapes and sizes. One major effect of this insistence on symmetry is a tendency for entrances to be centrally placed in buildings or pavilions, and in turn to generate an elevation having an odd number of bays, and hence an even number of columns; it is very rare and archaic for a major order to consist of an odd number of columns or pilasters.

2. THE PROGRESSION OF ELEMENTS

The progression of elements in a façade, from top to bottom, is closely controlled:

> Balustrade or blocking course
> Cornice
> Frieze
> Architrave
> Capital
> Shaft
> Base
> Pedestal

This is capable of a degree of manipulation; elements may be omitted or 'elided', expanded, for example where the pedestal becomes a basement or the blocking course an attic; in some circumstances elements like the frieze and architrave can be treated freely to correspond with the internal layout; orders may be superimposed, roof-storeys expressed on the elevation and so on. But the basic sequence cannot be distorted too far or it becomes meaningless. A column must have an entablature of some kind to support, and its capital must be at the top. Horizontally, a classical façade is essentially an assembly of repetitive elements with a recognisable simple or compound rhythm of bay-widths expressed by columns, pilasters or simply by the fenestration, and a degree of uniformity in the minor elements, such as windows. It follows that two orders should not be mixed except in the most specialised circumstances; an entablature supported by, say, both Corinthian and Doric columns would look unlettered. (To be fair, some of the greatest architects of the past have on occasion ignored this characteristic, with dramatic effect.)

It is worth bearing in mind in this connection that at its roots classical architecture is essentially an architecture of single-storey buildings, furthermore of buildings very simple in plan form. A great part of the development of classicism, and much of the interest of designing in a neo-classical style, arises from solving the problems of adapting the language to fit multi-storey buildings of complex plan.

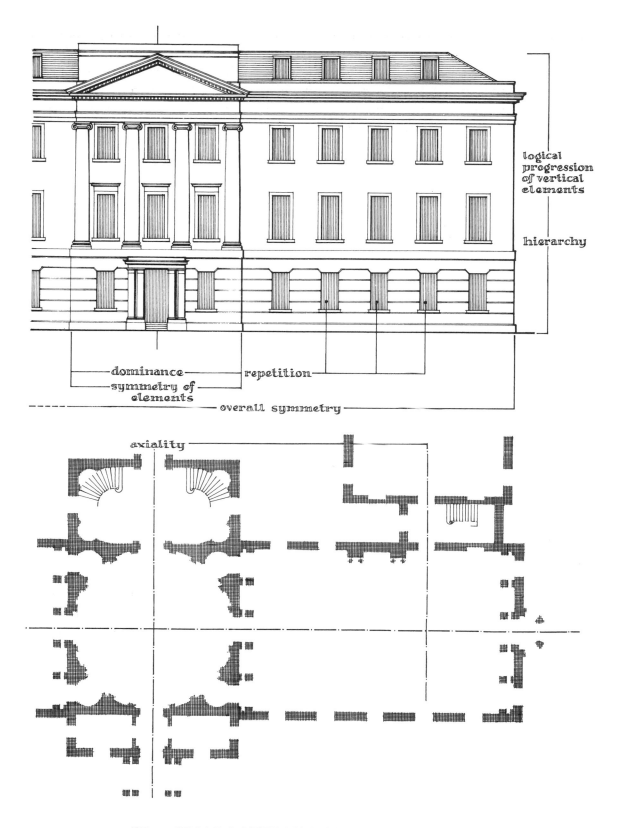

logical
progression
of vertical
elements

hierarchy

dominance
symmetry of
elements

repetition

overall symmetry

axiality

77.   CHARACTERISTICS OF CLASSICISM

205

3. THE HIERARCHY OF ELEMENTS

Just as there is a natural sequence of elements, so there is a tendency for a hierarchical nature to emerge in classical elevations, and indeed in plans. The dominant element will often be the giant order itself, and the effect of this can be considerably modulated in many ways: by alternating colonnades with pilasters, by confining the order to pavilions or to the centre, or by leaving the order entirely implied and emphasising the entrance with a columned porch. When the giant order is omitted, there is still a wide choice of methods of expressing a hierarchy, with an element dominating the whole. Plate 77, for instance, shows some ways in which a hierarchical character could be instilled by simply varying the degree of embellishment of the window surrounds.

4. MODERATION

It is, finally, a prime characteristic of classical architecture that it is not carried to excess. The style, it must be remembered, is derived from a comparatively unsophisticated method of building construction, using materials relatively weak in shear and thus confined to short spans, unless arches are introduced into the design. We have therefore seen that successive authorities laid down guidelines for column-spacings which generally restrict the bay-widths of a façade within narrow limits. Bays in classical façades tend to be significantly taller than they are wide, and window openings are almost universally portrait shaped rather than landscape. If this characteristic is not respected it is very easy for the classical flavour of a design to be lost. Likewise, cantilevers are unusual, being generally confined to projecting balconies, and of course to decorative elements such as cornices. There is, I suspect, also a limit to the number of storeys that can be accommodated within the compass of a classical façade without straining it too far, somewhere about six storeys including the basement. Attempts to spread the vocabulary over a bigger compass tend towards the grotesque.

Classicism, then, is not given to excess; it makes its effects with modesty and moderation, perhaps saving a note of exaggeration where some extra emphasis is justified. Its enduring satisfaction is that within what appears to be such a restrictive discipline, limitless variety of expression can be achieved without recourse to too many superlatives, yielding an unparalleled liberty in design.

GLOSSARY

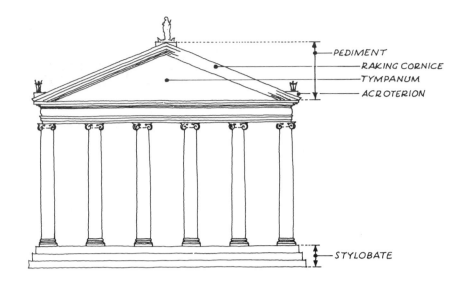

FIGURE 5   Parts of the order – stylobate and pediment

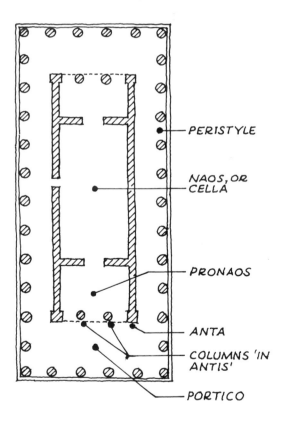

FIGURE 6   Terms used in the plans

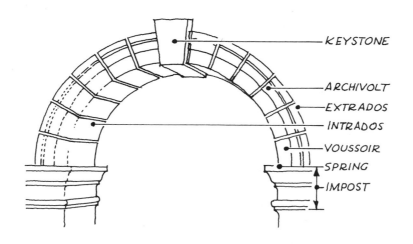

FIGURE 7   Parts of the arch

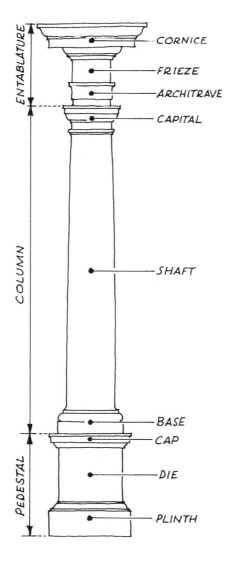

FIGURE 8   Main parts of the order

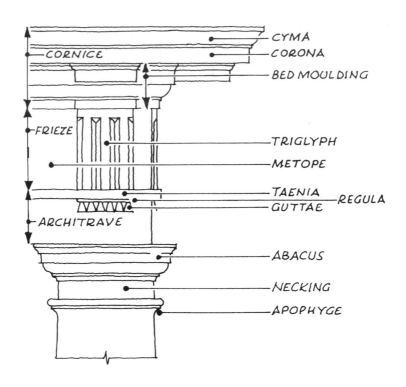

FIGURE 9 The Doric order

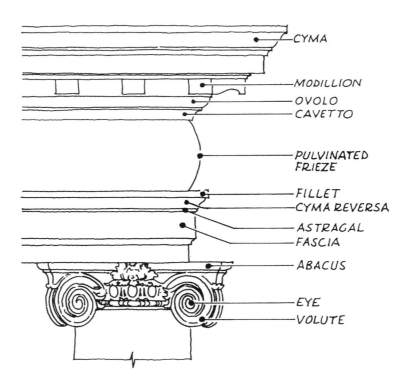

FIGURE 10 The Ionic order

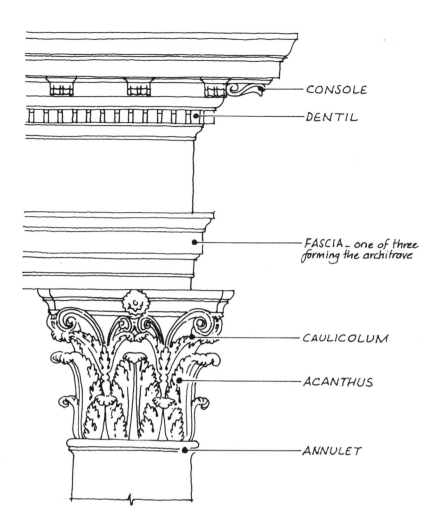

CONSOLE

DENTIL

FASCIA _ one of three forming the architrave

CAULICOLUM

ACANTHUS

ANNULET

FIGURE 11   The Corinthian order

ABACUS   The square slab crowning the capital and supporting the architrave; in the Ionic and Corinthian it is given concave sides and its mouldings may be enriched.

ABUTMENT   The solid mass flanking an opening which resists the thrust of an arch springing from it.

ACANTHUS   The multi-foliated plant which in stylised form is used to decorate the capital of the Corinthian order, and also to enrich mouldings, especially the ovolo.

ACROLYTHIC   Having stone or marble extremities; used to describe wooden statues with stone heads, hands and feet.

ACROTERIA   The small pedestals at the apex and extremities of a pediment which provide a level base for statues or other ornaments.

ADYTUM   The innermost sanctuary or shrine of a Greek temple.

AEDICULE   The architectural surround to a niche or opening generally consisting of miniature columns supporting an entablature.

AGORA   The public square or marketplace in a Greek city.

AISLE   The secondary open space to the side of the main nave of a building, separated from it by a colonnade or arcade.

AMORINI   Decorative figures of small, cupid-like children. Also called putti or cherubs.

AMPHIDISTYLE IN ANTIS   A temple plan having two columns between antae to front and rear, and plain walls at the sides.

AMPHIPROSTYLE   A temple plan having porticoes at both ends.

ANCONES   Projections left on blocks of stone for ease of handling during construction; consoles on either side of a doorway supporting an entablature.

ANNULET   A flat fillet moulding raised above the circumference of a column.

ANTA, ANTAE The Greek equivalent of a pilaster, in particular the end of a wall treated as a pilaster and responding to an order of columns, but usually with the capital and base differently treated from theirs.

ANTEFIXAE   The ornamental blocks covering the open ends of pantiles at the eaves, or placed as a cresting on a ridge, those at the eaves frequently taking the form of the head of a lion or other animal.

ANTHEMION   A continuous bas-relief ornament of alternating palmette and lotus or honeysuckle, all in stylised form.

ANTIS, IN   A portico plan in which the ends of the flanking walls project to range with the enclosed columns (and are often finished as antae).

ANTITHEMA   An undecorated, unmoulded block forming a backing piece to an architrave or frieze.

APOPHYGE   The cavetto connecting the shaft to the fillets which terminate it at top and bottom.

APRON   The panel beneath a window, sometimes fielded or adorned with bas-reliefs or other ornament.

APTERAL   A temple plan having plain walls at the sides, with no columns.

ARAEOSTYLE   A column spacing of 4 diameters between columns (5 diameters between column centres).

ARCADE   A series of arches supported on piers or columns. When the space between the piers is filled in with a wall the arcade is said to be blind.

ARCH   A curved structure composed of small bricks or stones, with radial voussoirs, which derives its stability from the wedge shape of the individual components. Arches may be circular, elliptical etc., and are capable of spanning larger openings than lintels.

ARCHITRAVE   The lowest of the three main divisions of the entablature, often divided into a series of flat planes and separated from the frieze by a plain or moulded band; a frame of similar profile round a door, or window.

ARCHITRAVE-CORNICE   An entablature consisting of architrave and cornice only, with the frieze omitted – a useful simplification for a subsidiary cornice.

ARCHIVOLT   An architrave moulding to an arch, following its curve.

ARCUATED   Having a system of construction dependent on the use of arches.

ARRIS   The sharp edge at the junction of two adjacent surfaces.

ASHLAR   Masonry constructed of stones dressed to a rectangular shape and laid in courses, as opposed to rubble work which is uncoursed masonry of random shaped stones.

ASIATIC BASE   The Ionic base evolved in Asia Minor, having a vertical-sided disc surmounted by a torus, both mouldings commonly fluted or otherwise decorated.

ASTRAGAL   A small-scale moulding of semi-circular section.

ASTYLAR   Without columns; without features that can be ascribed to a specific order.

ATLANTES   Carved male figures serving as columns to support an entablature – the male counterpart of caryatides – also known as telamones.

ATRIUM   A courtyard within a building and therefore enclosed on all four sides, but with the centre open to the sky, often with a surrounding colonnade like a cloister.

ATTIC BASE   A column base composed of an upper and lower torus, separated by a scotia with fillets, used with minor variations in all orders except the Tuscan.

ATTIC STOREY   An upper storey above the cornice of the principal order, and designed as part of the main elevation, sometimes with its own subsidiary order. Not to be confused with a roof-storey or garret-storey.

BALDACHINO   An open structure, normally placed over an altar to give it architectural emphasis, having a canopy supported by columns.

BALTEUS   The decorative band which appears to constrain the scroll on the end or baluster side of an Ionic capital corresponding to the volute on the face.

BALUSTER   A diminutive column supporting the hand-rail to a staircase or landing, a series of balusters being termed a balustrade.

BALUSTER-SIDE   The end or return face of a parallel-sided Ionic capital. Also referred to as the pulvinus.

BAR-BALUSTER   A baluster of plain section, usually either round or square.

BAROQUE   Literally misshapen, whimsical or grotesque, and hence used pejoratively in the past. Baroque describes a style of architecture derived from the mid-late Renaissance which rejected austerity and severity in favour of elaboration, enrichment and a degree of exaggeration.

BASE   The lowest element of a column or other architectural feature.

BASEMENT   The lowest storey of a building, usually plain and substantial and providing a solid platform for the order above.

BASILICA   A Roman building serving as a law court and assembly hall, to some extent derived from the Greek stoa, but totally enclosed; generally rectangular with nave and aisles, having an apse at one or both ends known as the tribune. Hence a prototype for a church.

BATTER   The deliberate inclination of a wall surface to give an appearance of great strength.

BAYS   Compartments into which the interior of a building is divided, separated by columns or pilasters and with transverse arches or beams similarly separating the roof. Each bay encapsulates the smallest repetitive element of the building and logically contains one window or composition of windows. Hence a façade showing a window repeated five times may be referred to as a five-bay façade.

BAY-LEAF GARLAND   A decoration of repeated stylised bay leaves.

BEAD AND REEL   A decoration of alternating, sometimes grouped, circular and oval beads generally small in scale and used to enrich the astragal.

BED MOULDING.   The moulding which supports a projection, for example the moulding or series of mouldings between the top of the frieze and the corona of the cornice above.

BELVEDERE   An open-sided structure at the top of a building which, like a gazebo, gives a vantage point from which to admire the view.

BLIND   Unperforated, for example an arcade built against a solid wall.

BLOCKED   Columns. Those in which the turned parts of the shaft alternate with square blocks; architraves similarly interrupted by plain blocks as in a Gibbs surround.

BLOCKING COURSE   A plain, square-edged course superimposed upon a cornice, on the plane of the frieze below.

BOLECTION MOULDING   A curved moulding covering the junction between a panel and its frame (e.g., in the construction of a door) and necessarily standing proud of both components.

BOND   The manner in which bricks or stone blocks are laid to restrict the vertical joints or perpends to a single course and thus produce a wall of the greatest strength. The resulting wall exhibits a regular pattern of stretchers (long sides) and headers (short sides).

BOSS   A decorative turned projection or knob.

BRACKET   A projecting member supporting a load, often formed of intersecting volutes and termed a console or modillion.

BUCRANIA   Carved representations of ox-skulls, often linked with swags and festoons to form the continuous decoration to a frieze, or used singly in the metopes of the Doric order.

CABLED   Fluting filled with a convex moulding, either plain or carved to represent a rope, usually confined to the lower part of a column.

CAISSON   A sunk panel in a flat or vaulted ceiling or lacunar.

CANALIS   The web connecting the fillets of the Ionic volute; in Greek Ionic convex, later concave in section, but more commonly flat in Renaissance examples.

CAPITAL   The uppermost element of the column, which visually gives support to the entablature.

CARTOUCHE   A raised panel or tablet of elaborate shape and often having a convex surface, with a decorative border normally curled like a scroll. The surface may carry an inscription, coat of arms, or other decoration.

CARYATIDES   Sculptured female figures serving as columns to support an entablature; the female equivalent of atlantes.

CASINO   A pavilion, summer house or pleasure house of ornamental character, often situated in the grounds of a larger house.

CAULICOLI   The leafy stems, or calyces, eight in number, which spring from the bell to support the angle volutes in a Corinthian capital.

CAVETTO   A hollow moulding, in profile either a quarter circle or a compound curve approximating to it. The cavetto generally links a plane or moulding to a broader plane below it. When it is reversed, with the projecting plane uppermost, it is termed a cove.

CELLA   The naos or enclosed chamber of a Greek temple.

CHAIR RAIL   A horizontal moulding running along a wall at roughly the height of a chair-back, which in theory protects the wall surface, though the chair rail itself is often enriched. Also termed a dado rail.

CHAMFER   The diagonal face where the arris is removed from the junction of two surfaces. It may be plane or hollow.

CHANNELLING   A form of rustication where only the horizontal joints between stones are emphasised by being recessed, the perpends being left flush.

CHRYSELEPHANTINE   A term applied to statues with faces, hands and feet of ivory, and armour or garments finished in gold.

COFFERS   In a ceiling, sunk panels, caissons or lacunaria.

COLOSSAL ORDER   An order of columns or pilasters embracing several storeys of a façade; also called a giant order.

CONSOLE   A carved bracket, having an S-shape formed of two volutes, that at the extremity is smaller than that at the base, frequently supported by carved acanthus leaves; used to support a projecting cornice in lieu of columns, and in the Corinthian cornice, beneath the corona.

CORNICE   The uppermost, projecting element of the entablature. Its practical function is to throw water clear of the work beneath. Its major components are the crowning cyma, the corona and the supporting bed moulding, but these are frequently elaborated with further ancillary mouldings as well as brackets, dentils, etc.

CORONA   The central component of the cornice, having a vertical face and horizontal soffit, often with a drip moulding.

CORTILE   The central courtyard of an Italian palazzo corresponding to the Roman atrium.

COVE   A concave moulding often large in scale, like an inverted cavetto, supporting the eaves externally, or raising the ceiling of a room above the cornice.

CUPOLA   A small dome, on a circular or polygonal base, roofing a turret and often finished with a finial or a lantern.

CURTAIL STEP   A step having its tread rounded at one or both ends on plan, at the foot of a flight of steps.

CYCLOPEAN MASONRY   A form of stonework originating in the Aegean, incorporating massive polygonal stones.

CYMA, CYMATIUM   A moulding in the form of a reverse curve, used as the crowning component of a cornice and elsewhere.

CYMA RECTA   A cyma moulding having a concave curve uppermost, with a convex curve below.

CYMA REVERSA   A cyma moulding having a convex curve uppermost, with a concave curve below.

DADO   The die or part of the pedestal of a column between its cornice and base; the lower part of a wall when treated as a continuous pedestal with the dado rail or chair rail treated as the cornice.

DECASTYLE   A ten-column portico.

DENTILS   Repetitive rectangular or tooth-like blocks worked on the bed moulding of a cornice of the Ionic, Corinthian or Composite orders.

DIASTYLE   A column spacing of 3 diameters between columns (4 diameters between column centres).

DIE   A dado, part of the pedestal, used especially to describe the rectangular block separating series of balusters in a balustrade.

DIMINUTION   The taper in a column from its base to its head, curved in profile and generally applied to the upper two thirds, the lowest third of the column being cylindrical. The diminution given in the metric plates is from a base diameter of 1 to a head diameter of 0.85.

DIOCLETIAN WINDOW   A semi-circular window divided vertically into three parts by two mullions, derived from examples at the Baths of Diocletian in Rome and therefore also referred to as a 'Thermae' window.

DIPTERAL   A temple form having a double row of columns on the long sides flanking the cella.

DISTYLE IN ANTIS   A portico having two columns set between antae.

DODECASTYLE   A portico of twelve columns.

DOME   A curved vault springing from a circular base, in section semi-circular (forming a hemisphere), segmental etc.

DORMER WINDOW   A window projecting from a pitched roof and therefore provided with a roof and diminutive walls (cheeks) of its own, lighting a roof-storey or garret.

DRESSINGS   Brickwork or stonework flanking a wall opening or adjacent to a corner, treated distinctly from the remainder of the wall face.

DRUM   A cylindrical structure upon which a dome or conical roof is raised to give it added emphasis; a cylindrical block of which a number go to make up a column.

EGG AND DART   A continuous decoration applied to the ovolo moulding, consisting of alternative egg shapes and darts or arrow heads, but with many variations and derived forms.

ENGAGED COLUMN   A column attached to a wall, but projecting by half its diameter or more, and therefore bolder in effect than a pilaster; also referred to as an attached column or an applied column.

ENTABLATURE   The uppermost part of an order of architecture, supported by the column and consisting of architrave, frieze and cornice.

ENTASIS   The curved profile of a column. The derivation from the Greek word for 'stretched' suggests a difference between entasis and diminution; the greatest diameter of a column with entasis occurs not at the base but at a point some distance above it. The difference between greatest diameter and base diameter is, however, very slight.

EPISTYLE   Greek term for the architrave.

EUSTYLE   A column spacing of $2\frac{1}{4}$ diameters between columns ($3\frac{1}{4}$ diameters between column centres).

EXEDRA   A recess in a wall, normally semi-circular on plan, large enough to accommodate a scat along its perimeter.

EXTRADOS   The convex curve of the outer edge of an architrave or other moulding applied to an arch.

EYE   The decorative central disc of an Ionic volute, sometimes enriched with a flower or other motif.

FAÇADE   The external elevation of a building, and especially its front elevation.

FANLIGHT   A window over a door and generally contained within the same frame. It is often semi-circular, having radial glazing bars resembling a fan.

FASCIA   A plain band with a vertical face: the architrave of the Ionic order has two stepped fasciae.

FEMUR   The raised section between the V-shaped grooves of the triglyph.

FESTOON   A swag; an ornament, generally in bas-relief, consisting of a garland of leaves, husks, flowers etc. suspended in a catenary from both ends.

FILLET   A narrow plain band with a vertical face, interposed between adjacent mouldings, e.g. on a cornice.

FINIAL   The decorative termination of a pinnacle, mast, spire etc.

FLEURON   The carved flower set in the middle of each face of the abacus in the Ionic, Corinthian and Composite capitals.

FLUTING   Repeated concave channels that maybe cut vertically into the face of the column in all orders except the Tuscan. In the Doric order they are normally separated by an arris, and in the other orders by a fillet.

FORUM   A public square in a Roman city flanked by the principal religious and official buildings, corresponding with the Greek agora.

FRET   An ornamental pattern of intersecting straight lines, forming a continuous band of decoration. Also termed a key pattern.

FRIEZE   The central element of the entablature, lying below the cornice and above the architrave, in the plane of the face of the column-head.

GADROONING   A kind of reversed fluting, consisting of repeated convexities often used to embellish decorative features such as urns.

GEISON   The Greek term for the cornice.

GIBBS SURROUND   A door or window surround extensively employed by James Gibbs, in which the architrave is interrupted by plain blocks.

GREEK CROSS   A cross with four equal arms.

GROIN   The arris formed by the intersection of adjoining surfaces of vaults.

GROTESQUE   A wall decoration of Roman origin, having human and animal figures interspersed with scrolls and foliage, to form a pattern rather than a pictorial representation.

GUILLOCHE   An ornament used to decorate a narrow band such as the soffit of a beam, consisting of a continuous interlaced pattern of sinuous curves, the circles left between them sometimes decorated with rosettes etc.

GUTTAE   The small drops shaped like pegs of conical section suspended from the soffit of the Doric mutule, and (in a single row) from the regulae in the architrave, corresponding with the triglyphs in the frieze.

HAWKSBEAK   A Greek moulding related to the cyma, curved on the outer face and undercut beneath; virtually absent from Renaissance work, but reintroduced by the neo-classicists.

HELICES   The diminutive volutes, sixteen in number, supporting the abacus in the Corinthian order.

HERM, HERMES   A bust (particularly of the Greek god Hermes) on a square pedestal generally tapering towards the base.

HEXASTYLE   A six-column portico.

HUSK   GARLAND A catenary-shaped festoon of husks or nut shells.

HYPAETHRAL   A roofless building or one with a central opening in the roof.

HYPOSTYLE   Having multiple rows of columns supporting the roof.

HYPOTRACHELION   In the Doric order, the horizontal grooves at the junction of the lowest part of the capital – the trachelion – and the top of the shaft.

IMPOST   The horizontal moulding or group of mouldings on a pier, serving as a capital, beneath the springing of an arch.

INTERAXIAL   The dimension between the centres of adjacent columns.

INTERCOLUMNIATION   The dimension of the clear space between adjacent columns: hence the interaxial = the intercolumniation plus 1 diameter.

INTRADOS   The curved soffit of an arch.

JAMBS   The sides of a door or window frame.

JIB DOOR   A hidden door. Flush panelled and designed to hang in the plane of the wall surface, it has the skirting and chair rail continued across its face and is decorated to match the wall.

KEYSTONE   The central wedge-shaped voussoir of an arch, often standing proud of its neighbours and emphasised by bas-relief or other decoration.

LACUNARIA   The sunk coffers in a ceiling.

LANTERN   A diminutive turret, circular or faceted, surmounting either a roof or a dome.

LATIN CROSS   A cross having three equal arms, and a longer fourth arm.

LINTEL, LINTOL   A beam spanning an opening.

LISTEL   A fillet.

LOGGIA   An area protected by a roof, behind an open colonnade or arcade.

LUCARNE   A small opening, with a gabled roof, in a roof or spire; a dormer window.

LUNETTE   A semi-circular window generally at high level in a façade, compositionally of less significance than a Diocletian window.

MANSARD   A roof divided into two pitches, the lower part steeper than the upper, derived from designs by the French architect François Mansart.

METOPE   The square space between the triglyphs of the Doric frieze, either left plain or decorated with bas-reliefs, e.g., bucranian masks, trophies etc.

MODILLIONS   The repeated diminutive brackets beneath the corona of the Corinthian or Composite cornice. The terms console and modillion seem to be generally accepted as synonymous, though there is a considerable difference between the orders, the Corinthian having scrolly brackets and the Composite square ones. In the text I have referred to the former as consoles and the latter as modillions, but this is a purely personal distinction.

MODULE   The basic unit of measurement for describing the proportions of the orders. Sometimes it is taken as the measurement of the column radius at its base, but more often as the base diameter of the column. Historically, the module is divided into either 30 or 60 parts or minutes.

MONOLITHIC   Of, say, a column when it is made from a single block of stone.

MUTULE   The rectangular block hanging from the soffit of the corona of the Doric order, immediately over the triglyph. It is the need to accommodate the mutule which gives the Doric its characteristically broad cornice projection.

NAOS   The cella or main chamber of a Greek temple, in which the statue of the god is accommodated.

NECKING   In the Doric order, the short section of plain shaft beneath the capital proper, and above the astragal and fillet marking the top of the main part of the shaft.

NEWEL   The post, generally square in section, which receives the balustrade hand-rail at a change of direction of a stair or landing; the central post or pillar of a spiral stair, often consisting of a series of drums carved integrally with the stair treads themselves.

NICHE   A recess in a wall, often semi-circular in section, to accommodate a statue or other ornament.

NYMPHAEUM   A building accommodating plants and flowers in a setting incorporating fountains or running water.

OCTASTYLE   An eight-column portico.

OCULUS   A circular window or opening set in a wall.

ŒIL-DE-BŒUF   A window similar to an oculus, but oval in form with the long axis horizontal.

OPISTHODOMOS   The room to the rear of the naos in a Greek temple, serving as a treasury chamber.

ORDER   The complete ensemble of column (or pilaster) and entablature, which may be extended upwards by means of blocking course, balustrade or attic, and downwards by means of pedestal and basement.

ORDER, IMPLIED   An order as above, having all the components in their proper juxtaposition, but with the actual columns omitted in favour of plain walling.

OVOLO   A convex moulding approximating to a quadrant, forming part of the bed mould-ing of the Tuscan capital etc. This moulding is seldom inverted.

PALLADIAN   MOTIF An arrangement of columns, favoured by Palladio, forming a triple opening, the arched centre opening being the widest of the three.

PALMETTE   An ornament consisting of stylised palm fronds disposed in a fan shape.

PANEL   The surface of a wall or door contained by the frame, commonly rectangular in shape and either flat or raised in the centre, i.e. fielded.

PARAPET   That part of a wall extending above a secret gutter and concealing gutter and roof; either plain, panelled, or balustraded.

PATERAE   Small applied ornaments, round in shape, sometimes enriched with flowers etc.

PAVILION   A projecting element several bays in width, often used to emphasise the centre of a building or the extremities of its wings.

PEDESTAL   An architectural device to increase the loftiness of a column, having a square die supported by a base and surmounted by a cornice on which the column base stands.

PEDIMENT   A triangular or segmental section of wall above the cornice of an order, and forming the end wall of a pitched roof, thus similar to a gable but generally thought of as being much flatter in pitch. The pediment is crowned by its own raking cornice, and beneath it the main horizontal cornice loses its cyma. Types of pediment include open and broken pediments, which have their cornices interrupted in the centre. Convention is con-fused as to whether a broken cornice is broken upwards, and an open cornice downwards – my own preference is indicated in plate 75.

PENDENTIVE   The curved, overhanging surface, a spherical triangle in shape, forming the transition between the circular springing of a dome and the polygonal entablature of a range of columns supporting it.

PERIPTERAL   Of a temple, having colonnades along the long walls of the cella.

PERISTYLE   A continuous colonnade around a temple; equally a peristyle can be turned inside out, being a colonnade around an open court, like a cloister.

PIANO NOBILE   The most important storey of a building – especially a palazzo – generally at first-floor level, expressed by the principal order which adopts the ground storey as a basement or podium.

PIAZZA   An open space surrounded by a colonnade, i.e. an enlarged peristyle, but follow-ing the completion of Inigo Jones's ranges of building in Covent Garden popularly used to describe colonnades or arcades themselves.

PIER   The vertical mass of masonry between two door or window openings and in an implied order taking the place of the columns; a similar mass supporting the springing of an arcade.

PILASTER   The rectangular shaft responding to a column, but attached to a wall. The pilaster may diminish like the column; its projection is never more than half its breadth, and normally substantially less. Sometimes the capital and base are identical with those of the column, but variations may also be employed.

PITCH   The angle between the slope of a roof or pediment and the horizontal.

PLATBAND   A broad fillet of shallow projection relieving the height of a plain wall, and often corresponding with an internal floor level.

PLINTH   The lowest element of the column base, generally a plain square slab (though Palladio sweeps the sides of the plinth into the top of the pedestal); likewise the lowest element of the pedestal.

PODIUM   A solid platform or continuous pedestal, on which an order is raised; a shallow basement.

PORTICO   The columned loggia in front of the entrance to a temple, or other building, frequently surmounted by a pediment, termed by the Greeks the pronaos.

POSTICUM   The loggia at the rear of a building corresponding with the portico. The enclosed area, behind the portico and in front of the naos in a Greek temple.

PROPYLAEUM   A building forming a ceremonial gateway.

PROSTYLE   Of a temple, having a portico in front only.

PSEUDODIPTERAL   Of a temple, having the peripteral colonnade spaced in relation to the cella wall as if there were two rows of columns, but with the inner row omitted.

PSEUDOPERIPTERAL   Of a temple, having pilasters or attached columns substituted for the flanking colonnades.

PTEROMA   The space between cella wall and columns in a peripteral temple.

PULVINATED   Of a frieze, bulging in a convex profile.

PULVINUS   The baluster side of a Greek Ionic capital.

PUTTI   Amorini.

PYCNOSTYLE   Having a column spacing of 1½ diameters between columns.

PYLON   A massive masonry structure pierced only by an entrance doorway, to which it gives great emphasis.

QUOINS   Rusticated masonry blocks placed to give emphasis to the corner of a building.

RAISED AND FIELDED PANELS   Panels having a raised area in the centre, connected with the plane of the panel by a moulding or a swept section.

RAKING CORNICE   The cornice along the sloping upper edge of a pediment.

REEDING   A series of parallel convex mouldings, resembling a bundle of reeds, applied to a flat or pulvinated plane.

REGULA   The short band corresponding to the triglyph above, placed below the taenia of the Greek Doric order, from which the guttae are suspended, possibly representing the pegged, protruding tongue of a tenon.

RESPOND   A half column or pilaster at the end of a colonnade and in line with the columns.

RETURN   The side or face of a surface or moulding at right angles to the main face.

REVEAL   The return of a wall surface into a door or window opening, normally at right angles to the main wall face.

ROCOCO,   ROCAILLE A form of Renaissance decoration, consisting of fan-shaped shell forms, scrolls and foliage etc. disposed in picturesque rather than symmetrical compositions, often in a very lavish manner.

ROSETTE   A stylised flower ornament, frequently applied to paterae.

RUSTICATION   Masonry of stone, brick or stucco with the joints between the blocks recessed with V-joints or other profiles imparting additional emphasis and visual strength to the wall.

SCAGLIOLA   A surface treatment of self-coloured plaster sometimes containing marble chips, applied to a backing and polished in imitation of marble, especially on columns.

SCOTIA   A concave moulding approximating to two linked quadrants, the lower of greater radius than the upper, used to separate the tori of the attic base and in balusters etc.

SCROLL   A volute.

SERLIANA   A Palladian or Venetian window.

SHAFT   The tapering cylinder of the column between base and capital.

SOFFIT   The underside of a projecting element such as a cornice, or any flat underside, e.g. of a beam or a canopy insufficient in dimension to be termed a ceiling.

SPAN   The clear distance between the piers or columns supporting a beam, arch or roof.

SPANDREL   The curved triangular wall surface bounded by the extrados of two adjacent arches.

SPLAY   A large-scale chamfer, such as a door or window reveal, wider at the wall surface than at the frame.

SPRING, SPRINGING   The point generally on top of an impost or column capital, from which the curve of an arch is developed.

STILTED ARCH An arch having a short vertical block between the top of the impost and the spring.

STOA An open space enclosed by colonnades, used by the Greeks as a public meeting place.

STOREY A horizontal subdivision of a building occupying a single floor.

STRING COURSE A horizontal moulding, either a flat fillet or of a more complex profile, run continuously along the face of a building.

STUCCO A plaster or cement rendering to the face of a building, either plain or with moulding and enrichments formed of the same material, often in imitation of stonework.

STYLOBATE The stepped podium of a Greek temple.

SWAG A festoon of leaves, husks or flowers represented as hanging from supports at each end.

SYSTYLE A column spacing of two diameters between adjacent columns.

TAENIA The fillet crowning the Doric architrave.

TERM A herm, having a bust supported by a tapering pedestal.

TESSERAE Small cubes of stone, brick or glass making up a mosaic.

TETRASTYLE A four-column portico.

TORUS A convex moulding of semi-circular profile, used especially in the bases of columns of all five orders.

TRABEATED A form of construction depending on flat beams spanning openings between piers or columns, without the use of arches.

TRACHELION The lowest part of the Greek Doric capital, separated from the top of the shaft by the grooves of the hypotrachelion, and from the spreading capital above by the annulets.

TRANSOM A horizontal frame between two window lights or between a door opening and the fanlight above.

TRIBUNE The apse at the end of a basilica; a raised gallery in a church.

TRIGLYPH The panel separating two metopes in the Doric frieze; it is universally divided by vertical triangular grooves into three narrow faces, and is said to be derived from timber construction representing a joist end.

TRIUMPHAL ARCH A free-standing structure, with a main central arch and subsidiary side arches, of a commemorative nature, and frequently adapted by Renaissance architects as a centrepiece to a composition.

TROCHILUS   Greek term for the scotia.

TROPHY   An ornament, generally carved in bas-relief, composed of weapons and armour etc. derived from the symbolic spoils of victory paraded in a Roman 'triumph'.

TYMPANUM   The triangular or segmental wall surface enclosed by the raking and horizontal cornices of a pediment, either plain or enriched with bas-reliefs.

VAULT   A continuous arch in the form of a segment of a cylinder, springing from parallel abutments to roof a building.

VENETIAN WINDOW   A triple window, the centre opening having a semi-circular head and flanked by subsidiary openings surmounted by flat lintels; the openings may be separated by plain piers or columns. Sometimes an outer, blind arch encloses the whole composition; a Palladian window, a Serliana.

VERMICULATION   A rough surface imparted to stone blocks especially in rusticated work, and supposed to resemble the multiple tracks of worms, although the 'tracks' are generally left proud of the remainder of the surface.

VITRUVIAN OPENING   A door or window opening decreasing in width towards its head, of Greek origin.

VITRUVIAN SCROLL   A continuous decoration in the form of waves with their crests curling over as if about to break.

VOLUTE   The spiral forming the major element of the Ionic capital.

VOUSSOIRS   The wedge-shaped stones forming an arch.

WEATHERING   The inclination of the upper surface of a cornice or other projection, designed to drain off water rapidly.

BIBLIOGRAPHY

1. The following books are quoted in the text and notes on the plates:

Sir William Chambers, *A Treatise on the Decorative Part of Civil Architecture*. Benjamin Blom's facsimile edn, 1968.

Robert Chitham, *Measured Drawing for Architects*. Architectural Press, 1980.

R. A. Cordingley, *Normand's Parallel of the Orders of Architecture*. Tiranti, 1959.

Sir Banister Fletcher, *A History of Architecture and the Comparative Method*, 1896 etc.

R. Fraser Reekie, *Architecture and Building Graphics*. Edward Arnold, 1946.

Terry Friedman, *James Gibbs*. Yale University Press, 1984.

James Gibbs, *Rules for Drawing the Several Parts of Architecture*, 1732.

Batty Langley, *The Builder's Jewel*, 1741. R. Donovan's facsimile edn, 1982.

Franz Sales Meyer, *A Handbook of Ornament*, Batsford, 1895.

Andrea Palladio, *I Quattri Libri dell'Architettura (The Four Books of Architecture)*, 1570. Dover facsimile of the 1738 London edn, 1965.

D. S. Robertson, *A Handbook of Greek and Roman Architecture*. C.U.P., 1929; 2nd edn, 1943.

Sebastiano Serlio, *The Five Books of Architecture*, 1566. Dover facsimile of the 1611 English edn, 1982.

Sir John Summerson, *The Classical Language of Architecture*. B.B.C., 1963; revised edn, Thames and Hudson, 1980.

Vitruvius, *The Ten Books on Architecture*. Dover, 1960.

David Watkin, *The Life and Work of C. R. Cockerell*. Zwemmer, 1974.

Mark Wilson Jones, *Principles of Roman Architecture*, Yale University Press, 2000.

2. Other books of particular relevance (apart from various Renaissance treatises referred to in the text) include:

Robert Adam, *Classical Architecture*, Viking, 1990.

J. J. Coulton, *Greek Architects at Work*. Elek, 1977.

James Stevens Curl, *Encyclopaedia of Architectural Terms*, Donhead, 1992.

W. B. Dinsmoor, *The Architecture of Ancient Greece*. Batsford, 1950.

Joan Gadol, *Leone Battista Alberti*. University of Chicago Press, 1969.

John Harris, *Sir William Chambers*. Zwemmer, 1970.

Alexander Speltz, *The Styles of Ornament*. Dover facsimile edn, 1959.

Rudolf Wittkower, *Architectural Principles in the Age of Humanism*. Academy Editions, 1973.